You Already Know

Hay House Titles of Related Interest

YOU CAN HEAL YOUR LIFE, the movie,
starring Louise Hay & Friends
(available as an online streaming video)
www.hayhouse.com/louise-movie

THE SHIFT, the movie,
starring Dr. Wayne W. Dyer
(available as an online streaming video)
www.hayhouse.com/the-shift-movie

* *

CYCLE MAGIC: Your Guide to Align with Natural Energy Cycles, Beat Burnout, and Manifest Your Dream Life by Elle Serafina

FOUR GIFTS OF THE HIGHLY SENSITIVE: Embrace the Science of Sensitivity, Heal Anxiety and Relationships, and Connect Deeply with Your World by Courtney Marchesani

THE PROMISE: Break Free from Limitation and Reclaim Your Inner Power by Mandy Morris

RECLAIMING YOUR INNER CHILD: A Journey of Childhood and Ancestral Healing by Nina Mongendre

You Already Know

STOP SILENCING YOURSELF, HEAL YOUR WOUNDS, AND TUNE IN TO YOUR INNER GUIDANCE

DANICA BANES

HAY HOUSE

HAY HOUSE LLC
Carlsbad, California • New York City
London • Sydney • New Delhi

Published in the United States by: Hay House LLC, www.hayhouse.com®
P.O. Box 5100, Carlsbad, CA, 92018-5100

Cover design: Kara Klontz • *Interior design:* Nick C. Welch

The author of this book does not dispense medical advice or prescribe the use of any technique as a form of treatment for physical, emotional, or medical problems without the advice of a physician, either directly or indirectly. The intent of the author is only to offer information of a general nature to help you in your quest for emotional, physical, and spiritual well-being. In the event you use any of the information in this book for yourself, the author and the publisher assume no responsibility for your actions.

Tradepaper ISBN: 979-8-3186-0125-5
E-book ISBN: 979-8-3186-0126-2
Audiobook ISBN: 979-8-3186-0127-9

1st Printing

Printed in the United States of America

This product uses responsibly sourced papers, including recycled materials and materials from other controlled sources.

The authorized representative in the EU for product safety and compliance is Penguin Random House Ireland, Morrison Chambers, 32 Nassau Street, Dublin D02 YH68, Ireland. https://eu-contact.penguin.ie

CONTENTS

This book is for the quiet ones, the ones who never felt like enough, who felt out of place, who shouldered the weight of those around them, strived to make no mistakes and convinced themselves they were fine. Keep walking the path home to yourself, one step at a time.

And for my daughters,
Life is a beautiful, imperfect unknown. Always have the courage to follow your heart, be true to yourself, and take up lots of space.

Introduction

The Collapsing

My heart was thumping out of my chest. Was that my heart? I felt like I was drowning, as if I was trapped and screaming for help, but my voice was on mute.

I was sitting on the kitchen floor, staring at a corner where the linoleum had hardened with time, causing it to crack and curl. The hiss of something bubbled on the stove above me. The screeches of glee from my children as they chased each other pierced my ears, and yet they sounded muffled, far away.

How did I get here?

This wasn't my linoleum floor. This wasn't even my house. Upstairs, our belongings spilled out of suitcases. I felt so out of place in my life and in my own body.

We had just moved back to New York from Singapore, in the middle of the COVID-19 pandemic, after living in Asia for four years. I felt the heat of my tears sting my eyes; the anger and resentment were burning a hole inside me. Pieces of me were collapsing, the story I had told myself about who I was and who I was supposed to be was crumbling, and all I could see was the cloud of dust rising around me. I was tired. My body was battling recurring infections. It was screaming for me to notice. I was screaming for someone to notice me, but it was the scream of someone who had already drowned: lifeless, inaudible. My voice wasn't there.

Had I ever had a voice, or was my voice just the echoes of everyone around me? I wondered.

What I didn't realize at this point was that I was going to have to let myself drown so that I could remember how to breathe.

You see, I had a secret. And the thing I was so afraid of, this secret, was the thing that was going to set me free. The thing that was going to help me find my voice and find my way home to myself.

I just had to let it out.

They say repatriating can be difficult—reverse culture shock, it's sometimes called. You return to a place, a home, where you think you'll seamlessly fit back in, but you've changed. The streets look the same, the shops are still there, and friends still see you as the person you were when they waved good-bye. But you now feel like an alien in this place you once knew so well.

It's a powerful metaphor for the process of awakening: a deep journey to your depths, a huge transformation, and an emergence as a whole new version of yourself, sometimes even unrecognizable.

I endured so many enormous transitions during those years away. Transitions I had been trying to tackle like I had always tackled things: with perfection. But I was starting to feel constricted in the life I had created, where I was so highly critical of myself, and everything needed to be "just so."

Sitting on that linoleum floor, it was as though the sand in the timer of living out my life in total misalignment had dropped its last grain. I didn't want to live like this anymore. I wanted so badly to be free. To be the person who showed up unapologetically as myself.

Maybe you've had a moment like this too, where everything you thought you were suddenly no longer fits, but you're not sure which way to go.

At the time, I was unknowingly emerging from a deep transformation, where I had uncovered parts of myself that had long been buried. It had been a journey of unbecoming and unraveling in order to remember who I was and step into my full, unapologetic self.

And that is, in a nutshell, what this book is about: my journey home to myself and how you, too, can begin to build a partnership with yourself, strong and rooted in connection. It's about remembering all the parts of us that make us who we are and embracing it all: the pain, the past, the anger, the truth, and the magic.

This journey involves listening to that little voice inside and learning to trust the cues of your body. In doing so, you can create more space for peace and increase your capacity to be not only at ease with yourself, but trusting and confident in yourself as well.

As women, we are often conditioned to abandon ourselves in subtle and not-so-subtle ways, starting from a young age. We're taught to shrink, to be less, to be agreeable, to conform to expectations of how we should look, sound, and behave. The clothes we are sold, the rules we follow, and the roles we are assigned can feel constricting. And we're taught not to complain.

As sensitive souls, we also experience a subtle layer of the world that most people don't, picking up on energies and emotions others often miss. Our heightened sensitivity can cause us to monitor, perhaps in a state of hypervigilance, the environments around us. Often, we end up absorbing external energies without realizing it, all of this leading to an increased state of overwhelm.

My own healing journey has been one of the most difficult but empowering experiences of my life. I often questioned why I didn't just take the shiny quick fixes that were offered to me. But deep inside, I knew that even those quick fixes would provide only temporary relief. I felt there was something more to uncover, a message in my own discomfort that wouldn't disappear with comforting Band-Aids placed on top. A message I could decipher if only I could learn the language of my body and inner wisdom.

In this book, I'll share the wake-up call that changed everything for me, what it taught me, and the process I used to build a deeper connection with myself and my body. I went from being terrified, unable to speak up for myself, afraid of my mediumship abilities, filled with rage and riddled with recurring health issues, to a professional psychic medium, intuitive guide, and author who now guides other sensitive souls to reconnect with their own intuition, their bodies, and their true power.

I think this is the part of the book where I am supposed to say I have found healing, and if you follow all the steps, you will too. While I have made tremendous progress in my personal healing journey by using these steps, I've also learned that healing is both highly individual and an ongoing process. With that in mind, I hope some (or all!) of what I offer you helps you on your own journey. Throughout the book, I'll offer invitations in the form of questions, reflections, and simple practices. Try what resonates and leave what doesn't. In Chapter 12, I offer you a framework to put together your own personal blueprint of practices that resonate with you and speak to where you are on your own journey.

In Part I: The Pull Inward, we'll begin our journey by exploring the call to change that often arises through life's challenges. Whether it's deep personal loss, entering parenthood, or major identity shifts, these deep transformations often come when we least expect them but offer us a chance to break free. In this section we'll confront the discomfort that arises from our unresolved wounds, we'll begin to question past beliefs and inherited narratives, and we'll look at both our light and our shadow. As we tune in and recognize this invitation inward, we set the stage for the deeper healing required to live a life that is true to us. As you navigate Part I, I encourage you to reflect on your own catalysts for change and awakening. What has called you to this moment? To this book? And what might happen if you allow yourself to enter the transformation waiting for you?

In Part II: The Four Core Wounds, I outline the four core wounds that I have identified as specific to highly sensitive women. These wounds might be playing a role in what is keeping you feeling disconnected or stuck. Whether stemming from societal conditioning, collective history, or patterns of protection, we look at the deep, often invisible, wounds that can affect highly sensitive women, and how these have shaped our relationship with our inner wisdom, voice, and personal power. We'll also examine the cost of this disconnection. This section is all about healing and reconnecting mind, body, and spirit. As you move through Part II, I encourage you to reflect on whether these four core wounds have helped shaped your own life. What patterns are you holding on to, and how can you start to heal your own relationship with mind, body, and spirit?

In Part III: Gentle Reconnection, we'll focus on moving into alignment with ourselves, reclaiming our true identity, and stepping into the power that we have always possessed. This section is about shedding old patterns, understanding and embracing our shadow side, and learning to trust the wisdom within. We begin by exploring *shadow work*, where we confront the hidden aspects of ourselves to break free from self-sabotage and uncover our true potential. Next, we'll dive into trusting our inner wisdom, distinguishing intuition from fear and building a deeper relationship with our internal compass. We'll end with a focus on reclaiming the power of our voice, finding the courage to express ourselves, our needs, and our boundaries. In the final chapter, I offer you a framework to put together your own personal blueprint for healing. As you navigate these chapters, I invite you to reflect on what practices speak to you most and how you can begin to incorporate them into your daily life.

Throughout this book, I'll refer to the universe, my inner wisdom, and universal wisdom. You may call these something else, perhaps Source, God, or your higher self. To me, they all represent the same thing. I encourage you to use whatever resonates most with you.

Above all, come to these pages with gentleness. If a practice speaks to you, try it. If it doesn't, feel free to skip it. Everything I discuss is simply an invitation. The most important lesson I want you to take away is this: Listen to yourself and your body. Trust in your own guidance above all. I chose *You Already Know* for the title of this book because you do already know. You have a divine connection that guides you in this lifetime. You may have forgotten that connection, but this book is about remembering deeply. The practices and insights in this book will serve as guides, but there is no one-size-fits-all path. As you explore and reflect on your own journey, you'll learn to trust yourself in ways you never thought possible and uncover the power and peace that lie within.

Because it's time, and you are ready.

Love,
Danica

PART I

THE PULL INWARD

Recognizing the Call to Change

In Part I of this book, I share my own unraveling as I walked through the portal of motherhood—the realization that so much of how I had been living was a performance of self-abandonment, and the toll it had taken on my mental and physical health. I explore how the pressure for everything to be measured and perfect, and the compulsion to control and contort myself, were manifesting as physical symptoms.

While I share my own experience and the research that supports how self-abandonment can have a physical and mental impact, keep in mind that this is one perspective and in no way medical advice—nor am I simplifying the experience of chronic health issues, as each of us will have our own experience.

As you read through this part of the book, perhaps begin to notice where you resonate with my own journey. Where might you be hearing the call inward or the call to change? Are you going through your own deep transformation? Do you find it difficult to speak up for yourself or share things about who you are?

This part of the book explores my own story, and call to change:

- The Entryway —realizing the discomfort is a call to change and uncovering layers of ourselves
- Breaking the Silence —why we shrink and silence ourselves as women
- The Invitation —the final message from spirit to take the leap
- Permission Slips —Maybe it wasn't the corn, maybe it was the people pleasing

In each chapter I share my personal story along with research and reflection questions for you to consider.

Let's begin.

✳ 1 ✳

The Entryway

They say when a baby is born, a mother is also born. But "they" never really tell you what that means. They'll tell you extensively about the heartburn and the hemorrhoids, but no one mentions that in nine months you will have to burn down the life you created and build from scratch a new life while you face all your inner demons, the things you had buried and forgotten. The past rises to the surface, saying, "Here you go, time to fix this" while you are simultaneously reading bedtime stories and just trying to provide love and stability for a child who sees you as their whole world.

Then there is a realization of your own stuff. The layers of hurt must either be addressed and handled or passed on in a neat little package to your child to figure out for themselves one day.

This realization hit me like a ton of bricks.

But it was only the edges of a realization. A sort of stepping into the light, squinting and blinking, trying to make sense of what was there to be witnessed. Your own inner child is crying out for the same attention your children are, and it's confusing and messy and hard as hell. No one has a pamphlet on how to raise your kid while you tend to your own pain and past. I found myself caught in the crossfire of wanting to do it perfectly and wanting to burn it all down.

It was an awakening.

Everything seemed all at once clearer than it had ever been, and at the same time, nothing seemed to make sense. *Why had I never noticed this before?* This was the beginning of what some call a "spiritual awakening." It was a deep and messy unraveling.

An awakening is often described as a deep transformation in our view and understanding of ourselves and our world. It involves a shift in our consciousness as well as our personal identity, bringing a deeper awareness of everything within us and around us. It can be an extremely turbulent and emotional process. We each will have our own calling inward, our own catalyst for change or entry to awakening. It might be the loss of a loved one, a serious health diagnosis, a near death experience, or the transformation into parenthood that calls you to begin questioning your choices. Whatever the catalyst is, it seems to become obvious that the way you've been living isn't working anymore, it's not serving you, and maybe it hasn't for a while. We might start to ask questions we never entertained before. Questions like *How did I get here*? Or *Why am I doing this*? These questions can jolt us out of the autopilot life we have been living, and we might have a subtle understanding that something needs to change, but we often don't yet know what or how, and it's a new awareness.

That was my experience.

On New Year's Eve 2015, I lost my sister, and before I even had a chance to process that she was gone, I found myself pregnant with my first daughter. Loss and new life were cracking the foundation of how I was living, pulling me inward and under. Then, shortly after my daughter was born, my husband accepted a job offer in Hong Kong. I simultaneously left my career and packed up our lives in New York to move to the other side of the world with our new baby. It was a blank slate in every sense of the phrase.

That move marked the beginning of my unraveling. It was an erosion of who I thought I was, as the masks I was wearing fell away, along with the stories I believed about myself. I slowly dismantled that identity, the one built on obligation, confusion, fear, and disconnection, until I finally reached my core.

The Process of Disappearing

In the world of expatriating, the partner who leaves everything behind and gives up everything to follow their spouse's career opportunities across the globe is referred to as the *trailing spouse*. This will probably not surprise you, but trailing spouses are overwhelmingly women and often struggle with isolation and loss of identity, which happen to be common themes in new motherhood and in spiritual awakenings.

I looked around our empty Hong Kong apartment. We didn't even have boxes to unpack yet. It was just me, my daughter, and our dog. My husband was already back in New York City on business. I stared around at the sheer blankness of it all.

How did I get here?

Here, I wasn't anything yet. No one knew me, and I could be anything I wanted. Be anyone I wanted. All the identities that assigned my worth up until that point had been stripped away. The promotions meant nothing. The certifications and degrees were on hold. The friendships held together by happy hours were too distant. If there was no longer a price tag attached to my name and no fancy title defining my value, what was I even worth?

Where did my worth come from?

A trailing spouse. . . . I thought about it. It was reminiscent of a lifeless piece of luggage: devoid of feelings or opinions, just along for the ride. *Have I always been a piece of luggage, trailing behind the voices and directions of others?*

I wondered if I had been a trailing spouse my whole life.

Out of Alignment

Standing in our empty apartment, I couldn't help but reflect on how the passivity of being a trailing spouse seemed to mirror how I had lived up until that point. I felt like a passenger in my own life. I wanted to understand why I felt this way. I wanted to understand the stories that helped shape what I thought was my place in this world.

Thinking back to my early childhood, I recalled how my parents always said that I was profoundly sad by the age of two. But the real truth, as I thought about it, was that I was a highly sensitive child in environments that were often overwhelming and unpredictable.

By age 14, I was having panic attacks and had been diagnosed with juvenile rheumatoid arthritis. By 16, I was drinking to black out and on antidepressants for diagnoses of generalized anxiety, major depressive disorder, and suicidal ideation. By 19, I was cutting myself. And by 22, I was starving myself, surviving on a bowl of oatmeal a day, abusing laxatives, and making myself puke when I felt out of control. I had been aggressively filling a void in me, masking my emotions and my opinions, and keeping myself ultra-busy, all as a distraction from something deep within.

Outwardly, I had been straightening and fighting my curly hair for decades. I was working out every day, sometimes twice a day, just to shrink my physical appearance. I lived an anxious dance between controlling what the outer world saw and numbing what my inner world felt.

From a young age, I had played the peacekeeper. I learned to fade into the background in an effort to take up as little space as possible, so no one had any added stress of worrying about me. I made myself and my needs unimportant. I learned to say, "I'm fine," when I was not fine, retreating further into myself, and I began the process of disappearing.

The Moment That Changed Everything

One afternoon, from a mattress pad on the floor of our Hong Kong apartment, I looked down at my daughter asleep on my chest. Her perfect chubby cheeks squished against me. I felt the gentle rise and fall of her breathing. I twirled the beautiful ringlet at the nape of her neck. Tears welled up behind my eyes. Not because I was sad that she had my curly hair in a world that would shove unattainable beauty standards in her face, but because I recognized, maybe for the first time, just how much I had detested my own curls.

Just how much I believed the lies about what was beautiful.

Just how much I loathed myself.

And I cried.

For all the times I had hurt my own body.

For the times I had been silent and small.

For the lies that became my story.

The lies about how I should look and act and feel and take up space.

The story that I was unimportant.

It was a moment of realization that brought me to my knees, face-to-face with myself. And as those tears burned my cheeks, they led way to space, a space that filled with the embers of rage. A rage I had never let myself feel before. If my daughter ever believed these lies about herself or forgot just how magical and powerful and beautiful she was, I would burn it all down.

In fact, I decided to burn it all down first, so she would never have to believe those lies.

I made the decision that if I was going to teach my daughter that the world would try to strong-arm her into abandoning herself, she would have to actively fight this coercion. Meaning, it was going to take a lot more than my words. I couldn't teach her that lesson while simultaneously straightening my curls, abusing laxatives, and saying yes when I wanted to scream "absolutely not."

I was going to have to learn this lesson while I taught it. Motherhood had opened this cavity in me that I had sealed shut tight. All the wounds I had been suppressing and ignoring, telling myself I'm fine, began to rapidly fester.

It was rapid-fire initiation.

Motherhood felt like a riptide pulling me out to sea. I was working to find and accept my new identity, all while grasping at old versions of myself that were no longer there. I wasn't even sure those versions were really me. The only way to survive was to surrender and let myself be dragged out with the current. To let go, so this new version of me could rise.

A Spiritual Awakening

Who am I?

It's one of the deepest questions we can ask in an awakening. Going through an awakening can feel a lot like you are losing your mind. Yet I think there is this glossy idea that a spiritual awakening is a process of divine connection, where we are experiencing signs and synchronicities and ease and flow, and life feels beautiful and expansive.

And while it definitely involves these perks, the heart of an awakening feels far less polished. It is the act of coming face-to-face with who we are, our shadow side, and our beliefs. And when we've been hiding from ourselves, this can be excruciating.

It's when the universe holds up a mirror and we decide to actually peek inside and witness the pieces of ourselves we haven't had the strength or the capacity to witness before.

It's when we begin to question everything we thought we understood about the world, who we are, and our place in it, letting the old pieces of us fall away so we can begin to rebuild in a more authentic way, in a truer way, without being driven by old patterns, fears, and conditioning.

It's seeing our raw humanness, and our scars, and understanding that they hold beauty. It's holding both the darkness and the light, understanding that one cannot really exist without the other. It's remembering that we are co-creators in our lives and finally taking the reins.

Our pull toward this waking up often begins with a profound sense of discomfort. This unease is a powerful signal that our current way of living no longer aligns with our evolving self. It's as if our soul is knocking, calling us to step into a transformation that is so needed.

We may find ourselves feeling completely out of sync, and our usual coping mechanisms or patterns begin failing us, no longer providing the comfort they once did. This misalignment can manifest in various ways, from physical symptoms like fatigue and stress to emotional turbulence. Overall, it can feel like we're in one giant funk.

It's as if we've been wearing distorted lenses our whole lives, and suddenly take them off, drastically changing how we see everything. This is when we start questioning everything we thought we understood, including what has been our truth. It feels as though our world has been turned upside down as we challenge these long-held beliefs, values, and patterns.

It's a time of intense self-reflection, often bringing a whirlwind of emotions: confusion, loneliness, sadness, and even anger, as old beliefs crumble.

All of it is valid.

All of it belongs.

We may also begin completely reassessing what matters to us; things that once seemed important—money, titles, success, material possessions—may now feel like a façade or completely unfulfilling. Instead, we're being driven by a desire for more authenticity, striving to align with our true self (our soul) as we navigate this transformative phase. While it can feel overwhelming, this questioning stage is a vital step toward our personal growth and a deeper connection not only to ourselves but to everything around us. This strive to better understand ourselves and move toward a more authentic way of living can feel like peeling back layers of who we are.

Our Many Layers

Sometimes we cannot fathom what is underneath until we unravel. We spend our lives shoving down emotions, reactions, truths in the name of conforming or keeping ourselves safe. And this coping might keep us safe for a while, but it can only take us so far.

Because we disappear when we use survival mechanisms. We erase ourselves. It's like we put on a cloak to blend in. And then one day, we realize we're still walking around with this cloak on that we didn't even know we were wearing. But our awareness of it makes it start to feel heavy, and we wonder if we're allowed to take it off.

If we're lucky, we find an environment where people love us, and they gently try to coax us out of the cloak, like children calling to a kitten to come out from under the couch. It's safe, they tell us. We just want to know you and love you. And we question them, because what if they don't love us when we take off the cloak? What if we're not safe?

I like this imagery of the protective cloak because it illustrates how, especially for those who have experienced trauma or deeply challenging situations, we adapt to survive, often at the cost of our connection to ourselves. But healing begins the moment we realize the cloak is optional. The journey of healing and personal growth starts with the task of rediscovering who we are under that cloak of protection.

✳ Questions for Reflection ✳

The following reflection questions invite you to begin exploring your own journey and what has shaped and influenced who you are. How have you been molded by societal expectations or family dynamics? Consider the stories you have been telling yourself, and try to determine if they are true.

1. How well do you know your true self, and do you let it shine?

1. I can't tell my true self from the stories I've taken on about myself.
2. I feel like I know who I am, but I often wonder if I am just performing.
3. I know who I am, but I only feel safe to show it when I'm alone.
4. I feel confident in who I am, and I show up authentically.

What ideas about yourself have you adopted that no longer feel true for you? Jot them down here.

____

____

2. Are you abandoning yourself to show up for others?

1. I can't remember the last time I thought about taking care of myself.
2. I don't even feel like I have time to take care of myself.
3. I feel like all I do is care for everyone else, and it makes me resentful.
4. I think I balance my care for others and my care for myself pretty well.

When taking care of others, are you doing it because you truly care, or is it more for control of the situation? Reflect below.

____

____

3. What areas of your life feel out of alignment?

1. In almost all areas, I feel like I am working against myself.
2. I feel like a lot of areas of my life are off, but a few are really solid.
3. Most parts of my life feel true and aligned for me, but there can be some improvement.
4. I feel like I am moving in complete alignment.

If you checked off mostly 1's or 2's for these questions, can you begin to reflect on why that might be?

____

____

Where did your limiting beliefs begin?

Many of the stories and limiting beliefs we tell ourselves were adopted from childhood or early experiences. Our caretakers' voices can become our inner critics. Where and when might these limiting beliefs about yourself have started? What is coming up for you as you explore this? Use the space below to journal some limiting beliefs you hold about yourself. Begin reflecting on if they're really true.

____

____

It's a Journey

The process of unraveling and shedding our layers may never truly end. The awakening I experienced was not an overnight revelation, but the beginning of a deeper, lifelong journey toward connecting to and showing up for myself. As I continued to dig beneath the layers of doubt, fear, and conditioned beliefs, I learned to see myself and trust myself.

There will be moments of discomfort, doubt, and confusion along the way. But there will also be moments of clarity, of releasing the old stories that no longer serve us, and of stepping more deeply into connection with ourselves. As you move forward, know that taking this path, however messy and imperfect, is a step to live with more connection, magic, and inner peace than you ever thought possible.

The way forward is inward.

In the next chapter, we'll explore the effects of self-silencing in women and how girls are often taught to be quiet, agreeable, and emotionally restrained. We're taught to prioritize others, often at the cost of ourselves, and we'll look at the impacts of this on a physical, mental, and spiritual level. Through personal reflection, research, and client experiences, I highlight the deep cost of self-silencing.

2

Breaking the Silence

"That's not very ladylike," I was often told growing up. I didn't really know what it meant, but I received this reproval when I was expressing anything in an outward manner: anger, an opinion, disapproval, a boundary . . . even a bodily function.

As girls we are socialized from birth to be polite, to be agreeable, to be quiet, and to forever be smaller. We're taught to suppress our appetite, suppress our rage, suppress our tears. We're taught to override our bodies and our sense of knowing in order to appease others and not ruffle any feathers.

We are taught that our boundaries are negotiable.

How many times have you given someone a hug even though your body was giving you a clear "No" signal, but you felt like it would be rude not to?

In school, we're taught to sit still when our bodies want to move. We're sexualized before we even sprout breasts. Over and over, we're taught to abandon ourselves in the service of others.

From our very first day of menstruating, we're taught that pain is normal, and we should push through it to keep showing up. We receive this message over and over to silence ourselves and our pain.

I remember going to my six-week checkup after my daughter was born. I was dealing with significant numbness and pain in my abdomen from an emergency cesarean section. My daughter was a colicky baby, so I was surviving on no more than 45 minutes of sleep at a time. When my midwife checked me out, she told me everything was normal and cleared me to have sex, casually suggesting I have a big glass of wine beforehand because it was going to be painful.

What?

Why do we treat women this way? Why is our pain something to suppress, to numb, just so we can keep showing up for everyone else?

I received that message loud and clear.

I started menstruating at age 14, and the pain was impossible, so severe it would often make me pass out or vomit. Within a year, I was prescribed painkillers just to make it through school, and no further testing was done. By age 18, I was put on birth control. My period became something I just learned to manage; pain was part of the deal.

If you remember from the previous chapter, I also had panic attacks, juvenile rheumatoid arthritis, anxiety, and depression. But by my 20s, I was dealing with chronic urinary tract infections and yeast infections, which persisted, almost cyclically, for the better part of a decade. A cycle that brought me to my breaking point.

More than anything, I just wanted to understand why. Why did I seem so prone to illness when others weren't? Over time, and after little relief from conventional medicine, it began to dawn on me that my tendency to shrink myself and people-please might be playing a role.*

The Cost of Silence

In 2022, I set out to conduct my own research on the physical effects of suppression and people pleasing. Along with my research, I interviewed women who self-identified as empaths or highly sensitive and who were also living with chronic or recurring health issues.

The conversations all went exactly the same.

Below are a handful of stories these women shared with me, though names and details have been changed to respect their privacy.

Angela, a highly sensitive mom who suffered with anxiety and a digestive disorder, had spent her whole life trying to control her world, to be the perfect wife and mother, always neglecting her own needs and even her health to prioritize others. When she did go to see a doctor, they could never provide an answer for her ailments.

Michelle, a highly sensitive and intuitive mom, was struggling with weekly migraines and a persistent bacterial infection. She was living every day in pain while swallowing her emotions in a family environment that didn't feel safe for authentic expression.

Liz, an intuitive empath, was dealing with inflammation, anxiety, and chronic stress. She felt she was always taking on others' emotions and lacked the necessary boundaries to support herself. She felt like she was drowning.

Ellen, a highly sensitive and introverted empath, was dealing with persistent illness, in and out of tests, and on and off medications. She was always worried someone would get mad at her and therefore constantly extended herself beyond her own capacity.

Simone, who had a laundry list of health issues, identified as a perfectionist people-pleaser who was raised to serve everyone else and was also hiding her own mediumship abilities from the world.

These women were all highly sensitive, intuitive, empathic, highly driven women who identified as having people pleasing and perfectionist tendencies with continued health issues. They were holding on to anger, they were never taught how to set boundaries, and they were struggling with unexplained chronic symptoms.

I resonated with their stories because they were also my stories.

In a recent article published in *Time* magazine, Maytal Eyal, a psychologist drawing on research conducted by Dana Jack, explored the connection between self-silencing in women and its potential impact on long-term well-being.

In the article, she noted that women account for close to 80 percent of autoimmune conditions and statistically are more likely than men to experience issues such as IBS, migraines, and fibromyalgia. Women also report higher rates of experiences like anxiety and depression.

Eyal goes on to suggest that the traits society often values in women, such as agreeableness, caretaking, and withholding any anger or emotional outbursts, may actually contribute to increased stress in the body over time. This article stopped me in my tracks because it was something I had already noticed in myself.

Drawing on Dana Jack's work from the 1980s, Eyal highlights how cultural expectations around femininity and self-silencing have been linked, in many studies since, to emotional strain and even physical health challenges. These findings suggest that the pressure to suppress our authentic selves can shape our overall well-being more deeply than we may realize.

It was a correlation I had noticed in myself and in those women I interviewed. This suppression of ourselves and the effort to restrict everything inside us for the benefit of others not only manifests in our mental health, but in physical illness as well. We'll get more into the physical aspects of this in Chapter 7.

As I close this section, I want to emphasize that although I've discussed research and my own experiences around how self-suppression may influence health patterns, chronic conditions are complex and influenced by many factors. My aim is not to oversimplify or make any medical claims, but to provide one possible lens and invite reflection.

The Realization of My Own Patterns

Five months into our new life in Hong Kong, just after my daughter's first birthday, I had a knowing from within. So, while the rest of the house was asleep, I peed on a stick. I was pregnant!

We were going to have two kids under two. Which felt both crazy and exciting. My husband, in his excitement, wanted to share the news with everyone. I was excited, but I also felt cautious, remembering my first pregnancy.

With my first pregnancy, I had peed on three sticks over the course of a month, and they were all negative. But my period was late for the first time in my life, and I just knew something was up. Eventually, I took myself to my primary care physician to see what was going on, and of course, the first thing she had me do was pee on another stick.

"You're pregnant!" she said as if it should have been obvious. "What sort of sticks *had* you been peeing on?" she asked while we laughed and hugged. Doing the math, we calculated that I must have been 10 weeks pregnant already, which was mind-boggling.

I made an appointment right away to see my midwife, but when I got in the following week, the news wasn't as exciting. "There is no heartbeat, and the amniotic sac is very small for 10 weeks' gestation," she informed my husband and me.

Everything in my body felt like it was sinking.

She told me to come back in the following week for more bloodwork to check on my HCG levels but to be prepared that I was miscarrying. I went home to wait in a limbo. We had been so excited, and now there was just fear on the edges of heartbreak. That weekend, I was scheduled to go away for a family member's bachelorette celebration. I was part of the wedding party, so I knew I had to go.

Did I have to go?

I never even considered choosing to take care of myself over meeting obligations and the expectations of others. It literally never crossed my mind. The only thing I felt was resentment that I needed to do something that felt impossible in the moment.

I thought about the general advice given to pregnant women regarding not sharing the news until you reach 12 weeks of gestation. It seemed like an odd rule. *Who does that benefit?* If you do experience a loss, are you supposed to just carry that grief all alone?

I didn't want to ruin everyone's celebratory wedding vibes with my sadness, so I shoved my fear and pain down to that place inside of me that seemed to be growing and bulging with unease and resentment. I put on a smile, and I just pretended to slam shots of vodka at the bar, letting them spill over my shoulder, making wooing noises, while my body felt exhausted, and my heart was breaking.

I pretended.

I suppressed.

I proudly wore the cloak that said I was easygoing and low maintenance.

And I overrode my body, my emotions, and that tug from my inner knowing, to show up for others. Because that's what I thought I was supposed to do. I still didn't realize I was doing it: this pattern of suppressing, this pattern of elevating my own discomfort in order to avoid letting others down and keeping everyone around me comfortable. I didn't realize I was constantly swallowing my thoughts and opinions and crossing my own boundaries. I was just on autopilot, living in the way I had learned to live and to survive.

We were lucky with that first pregnancy, and nine months later, my beautiful baby girl was born. But now, sitting in the morning light of our Hong Kong apartment, looking into my husband's eyes, I remembered that fear from the first time around, that heartache of what could happen, and still not realizing my pattern, I asked him, "Please, can we just wait? What if something happens?"

Don't let people too close. It's safer by yourself. These were my mantras. I was quite comfy managing things on my own. It felt easier that way. It was easier for me to manage my hurt than to be vulnerable enough to let others hold space for me.

Until it wasn't.

The thing about the fringes of an awakening is you will start to notice that how you have been living isn't actually supportive of you. Your discomfort feels deeper; the nudge from within gets louder, asking you to notice how you aren't being true to yourself. The universe holds up that mirror again, and something in you stirs, whispering, *Please.* But you're afraid, afraid to let go, afraid of the unknown. Why does our discomfort feel so much more comfortable than choosing something new for ourselves? Transformation is bubbling under the surface, and it's getting harder and harder to keep that lid on.

The Patterns

As highly sensitive women, we are susceptible not only to the messages of how we should behave, but also to the responses from others that we feel so deeply: their disappointment, the subtle shifts in energy or facial expressions. Very often we want to avoid letting others down or causing conflict, so we prioritize others above ourselves.

Call it my psychic abilities or just mother's intuition, but deep in my heart I already knew I was going to lose this baby. "Dan!" I heard myself scream. He ran into the bathroom. "I'm bleeding," I half-shouted as I fell, shaking, into his arms.

It was Saturday morning, and we had several interviews lined up to meet with possible babysitters. Crying, I heard the loud swish of the toilet flushing behind me.

What does one do when they are having a miscarriage? Call the doctor? Drive to the hospital? Nothing? I wasn't sure. I felt overwhelmed. I didn't know anything about the hospital system in this country yet. I just wanted to curl up in bed.

My phone dinged, bringing my attention back into the moment. It was a text message from one of the babysitters we interviewed earlier that morning. Everything felt blurry, like my body was going through the motions without me in it. I was spreading peanut butter on crackers for my daughter when the next interviewee showed up.

When one is having a miscarriage, I suppose one just continues to go about one's day while they completely fall apart inside, losing everything.

And honestly, that is how life often felt to me.

Like all I was doing was making everyone something to eat while I screamed on the inside. No words to ask for help. No clue how to state out loud what I needed (did I even know what I needed?). Just bottling stuff up and checking off the list of expectations while I was drowning myself.

Understanding Why

As women, from the time we're toddlers, we're handed dolls, strollers, and bottles and expected to know how to care for others. We receive constant reinforcement for how polite we are, how good we are, and how agreeable we are.

When we raise our voices, we're called angry. When we assert our needs, we're called aggressive. We seem to only ever be surviving in a patriarchal system that thrives off our silence. We are expected to be submissive, to follow the rules, to share our bodies.

The pressure to shrink into these restrictive ways of living limits our ability to express our full range of emotions and our authentic selves. It limits our ability to even know ourselves. This shrinking is keeping energy, words, and truths stuck in our bodies with nowhere to go.

In one 10-year study that looked at 3,000 women, the ones who self-identified as almost always censoring themselves or remaining quiet in conflicts had the highest risk of premature death.

Silence becomes like a slow poison.

After I lost the baby and didn't tell anyone about it, this rage began boiling inside me. I was so angry. I was angry that no one was there to console me (how could they be? I didn't tell them). I was angry at people who didn't know what I was going through. I was angry at my body for letting me down. I didn't know it yet, but this anger was going to be the invitation inward.

Very often the anger we feel, or the resentment pulling us under, is asking us to notice where we aren't expressing our needs and our truth. It's an invitation to show up for ourselves. The major life experiences of losing my sister to cancer and becoming a mother within a year of each other, then losing the baby, were a tornado propelling me into my own awakening. It tore away the very foundation I had built my life on. I would eventually realize that foundation was never a stable support anyway, and it was time to rebuild it. It was time to decide who I was and what I wanted from my life.

In a world that often asks women to shrink, to be polite and more agreeable, we can lose sight of our truth—of who we are on a soul level. For so long I silenced myself, not just in the wake of my miscarriage, but in countless moments throughout my life where I put others first, ignored my own needs, and suppressed my voice. But the cost of our silence is a high price. It's not just the physical and mental; there is a spiritual cost; it's our soul cost. The anger, grief, resentment, or frustration we carry beneath the surface is a message. A message that something is not aligned, something is off and needs our attention.

This tendency to self-silence is not just a conditioned response; it's often a survival mechanism that, over time, erodes our sense of who we are. Finding our voice and reclaiming this part of ourselves is not a simple task. It asks us to risk disappointment, to risk conflict, and sometimes, even to risk losing relationships. Those are big risks. But our power lies in our voices. And in embracing all of who we are: our patterns, our anger, our grief, and welcoming them in instead of hiding them. This is how we make a change.

✳ Questions for Reflection ✳

1. Do you feel like you tend to swallow your voice instead of projecting it?

1. I don't share my thoughts or opinions or feelings. Ever.
2. If I try to share something, I break out in a sweat and my voice is shaky.
3. I am usually comfortable to share but sometimes overthink it later.
4. I feel comfortable sharing my truth, feelings, and needs.

If speaking is difficult for you, get curious about why. When in your past might you have felt silenced or afraid to speak up? What is holding you back from speaking up now?

____

____

2. What would you need to change in order to begin sharing your needs, ideas, or truth?

1. I don't feel like I'll ever be able to do this.
2. I want to change, but the changes are so big, they feel overwhelming.
3. I know what I have to change, and I've started taking steps.
4. Speaking up and using my voice come pretty easily for me.

What sort of fears come up when you imagine voicing your needs or truth? What sort of hopes? Take note of what you feel in your body when you imagine sharing your voice.

____

____

3. How comfortable are you with expressing emotions like anger, grief, or frustration?

1. I avoid expressing these at all costs.
2. When I do express these, I often feel guilty or ashamed afterward.
3. I express these emotions sometimes, if I feel safe, but I often second-guess if I was right to do so.
4. I have a pretty healthy relationship with anger, grief, and frustration.

What would happen if you welcomed your anger and just gave it some space within you?

____

____

If you checked off mostly 1's or 2's for these questions, can you begin to reflect on why that might be?

____

____

When Did Your Self-Silencing Begin?

For many women, self-silencing is a deeply rooted pattern. We might not even realize we are doing it. Reflect on where you might deflect to others to make decisions. Maybe your partner asks what you want for dinner, and you'd rather they choose. Or a friend asks what movie you should watch, and you tell her to pick. When do you choose to keep the peace over speaking up? You might feel really strongly about something, but your family feels opposite, so you don't share your thoughts. Write freely here or in your own journal.

____

____

____

____

Key Takeaways

As women, self-silencing can feel like a way of life, whether it was the message we received from society or simply what we witnessed our own mother do when we were growing up that became our learned behavior. As you begin to become aware of and decondition yourself from these restrictions and start to challenge societal norms, allow yourself to focus inward, touching on the pieces of you that would like to be noticed and seen. Start by exploring what might be contributing to your fear of sharing parts of yourself or asking for what you need. Perhaps it's your sense of self-worth or fear of what others may think or say. We will get into more of the core wounds that shape this pattern in Part II of this book, but as you begin to peel back your own layers, you may find that this journey leads you into the darker corners of yourself. These are usually where our deepest wounds reside, the parts of us we've kept under lock and key. This depth can be an uncomfortable place, but it's also from this space that we can begin to truly witness ourselves and hear our soul's call.

In the next chapter, we'll discuss the dark night of the soul, or what I like to call the Goo phase, where we dissolve illusions and old ways of thinking into a goo, like a caterpillar entering a cocoon. It's a time of reckoning, where we begin to face our shadows, and sometimes, our deepest fears, and it opens with the secret I kept hidden most of my life.

✳ 3 ✳

The Invitation

Gradually, and all at once, you will hear it.

A whisper that says: “It’s time.”

No more dimming. No more hiding.

It’s a whisper of truth you’ve always known.

And yet you will wonder how you haven’t heard it before.

But it will be impossible to ignore any longer.

My dear, you were never meant for small
and cramped spaces.

You were meant to breathe life in.

It will ask more of you, this voice. But you are ready.

So let it all crack and crumble, and know

you are ready.

Even when fear clouds your path.

Even when you cannot see ahead of you.

Because you are awakening, and your soul is
calling out to you.

My earliest memory of interacting with a being from the other side was when I was five years old. I was in my childhood bedroom, which was a converted attic space I shared with my younger brother, when the ceiling completely disappeared, and a figure hung in the sky above me. It was surrounded by the brightest light I had ever seen, a white that pierced my eyes. This being didn't say anything to me, but I remember feeling a wave of intense awe and love wash over me, like nothing I had ever felt before. And then it was gone, and fear set in.

Even as a child, I didn't tell anyone what I saw; I already knew it would likely not be believed. As the years went on, I would see more beings and hear them whisper, like many voices talking at once, but I could never understand what they were saying. I would sometimes simply see floating faces in the room with me, which as you can probably imagine, always freaked me out. I would tell myself I was just being silly, or that didn't just happen. I would often know things without understanding how I knew. In fact, I remember a dream I had one night where we were walking in the woods as it was getting dark. My dad was several feet ahead of me with his back turned. The energy felt foreboding. I saw him clutch his chest and drop first to his knees, then backward onto the forest floor. I screamed and raced to him, but I couldn't move; I couldn't get there. Then I woke up, heart racing, tears running down my cheeks.

I was breathing heavy, trying to calm myself down. *It was just a dream*, I thought. But last time, it wasn't just a dream.

The house was dark and still as I stepped out of bed. The red numbers on the clock informed me it was 3:00 A.M. My dad's room was only across the hall; I opened my door and could already see he was not home. His bedroom door was still open; I peeked in just to be sure. He sometimes got home late, but this felt very late. I told myself it was fine and got back in bed, pulling the covers up over my head, curling into a ball. The energy of the dream, the intensity, was still sitting with me.

It turns out that night my dad had driven himself to the hospital for chest pain.

This might all sound really cool, but at the time, none of this stuff made sense to me, and it all felt really alarming.

Duality

When I was 24, I moved into my first apartment, a small studio where I lived alone for the first time in my life. At the time, I was balancing a very demanding schedule. I was enrolled in a master's program, attending classes at night while working full-time during the day. On my days off, I was fulfilling my internship hours. On top of all that, I was navigating a relationship with my now-husband, who lived almost two hours away. I survived on caffeine and alcohol, and I was busy in every sense of the word.

I kissed my parents good-bye and closed the door behind them, turning to look at my one-room space. I liked it. But almost immediately, something felt off. When the sun dropped below the horizon, I no longer felt alone in the space.

Of course I am alone, I told myself. *I am living in one small room; I can see every corner at the same time.*

I closed my eyes to fall asleep that first night, and that's when it started.

It began subtly, lights flickering, the sound of whispers in the quiet of night, figures appearing at the end of my bed. Sometimes I felt the weight of someone sitting on my bed, shifting the mattress down. My electronics would act up without explanation; my laptop would power on and off by itself. My toilet would flush by itself. I would hear my name being called and the sound of my front door opening. These occurrences happened several nights a week and continued for what would ultimately span the next five years.

Being raised Roman Catholic, my family and I had gone to church every Sunday. We said our prayers before bed every night and grace before dinner. We had a crucifix in every room, with rosary beads and holy water scattered throughout the house. We were taught to believe in God and heaven and hell. Anything that didn't fall under the holy, fell under the unholy.

Which I was pretty sure was where speaking to ghosts fell.

Aside from the religious considerations around mediumship, my only exposure to the paranormal was the Hollywood depiction of possessed people crawling backward up walls in dark rooms while creepy music played. Scary stuff. I didn't like scary stuff, and I was a pretty strict rule follower, so naturally I was afraid of my own ability as a medium.

My Fear Kept Me Stuck

Within that first month of living alone, as my mediumship abilities suddenly sprung wide open, was when the recurring infections started.

I didn't tell anyone what I was experiencing. Part of me feared that speaking about it out loud would make it worse, like how saying Beetlejuice three times would summon the chaotic ghost in the movie *Beetlejuice*. But mostly, I was afraid of what people would think. They would definitely think I was crazy. I would be deemed unfit to work in mental health, and they would kick me out of my counseling program.

Perhaps you've had moments in your own life where you kept something inside or hidden for fear of being judged or ridiculed. And if so, you know the grip it can have on you. These fears kept me silent. At the time I didn't make the connection, but my fears were actually keeping me silent about a lot. I was operating in a constant state of stress, trying to hold everything together while completely overriding my body and ignoring spirit. This duality seemed to define my life. On the outside, I worked hard to fit into society's mold of normalcy; on the inside, I fought an invisible war with myself and my body.

My sleep suffered immensely, and my urinary tract and yeast infections became a part of my life. I was feeling like a tired husk of a person. I was in and out of doctors' offices, nodding along as they said things like:

"Make sure you wear cotton underwear."

"Don't wear clothes that are too tight."

"Make sure you're peeing after sex."

I was doing all of these things, religiously, but it didn't matter. I would nod in agreement and walk out with my prescriptions.

Speaking the Truth

Weeks turned into months turned into years. I was desperate for help, but I didn't even know who to turn to. But that would change when Dan's lease was up, and we decided to move in together. And by *in together,* I mean into my tiny studio apartment.

Dan is the one person on this earth who knows me, everything about me. My past, my heart, he can see right through my tough exterior. But at this time, I had never shared with him the fact that, at night, ghosts showed up to flush my toilet. Wasn't really sure how to squeeze that into a conversation.

But it was time.

I had to tell him what was happening to me. With hands shaking, and a familiar flush across my chest, I asked him, "Can I tell you something?" wondering how this information would be received. Wondering how to find the words to not sound like I'd gone off the rails. It felt like so much was weighing on this truth.

I had an amazing relationship; I had a career in the mental health field. What if I lost it all by sharing this?

Dan is not the flustering type. He is steadfast and logical.

"Anything," he responded. "What's up?"

I was fidgeting with my shirt sleeve as I thought about how to explain it.

I see dead people?

The apartment you just moved into is haunted?

I decided to just start at the beginning and walk him through everything. To my surprise, he was not repelled or afraid, but instead curious, and more than that, he believed me. I felt relieved to have said it out loud.

Turns out, not only did Dan believe me, but he knew of a spiritual healer in his hometown who might be able to help.

And that's how I found my way into the office of Pat Longo, a renowned spiritual healer and teacher.

I remember sitting down on the couch in her office and looking around as she gathered some things, talking to herself out loud, or to me, I'm not sure. She was discussing what a week it had been!

The room was like any other room, with pictures and books and knickknacks. I noticed a picture of Jesus and wondered if she was Catholic. *Can you be Catholic and spiritual?* I thought.

I was clinging to a pillow I had placed on my lap and trying not to be too weird.

"So!" she said, taking her spot in the huge armchair adjacent from me. "What brings you in today?"

Um, where do I begin?

The inaudible voices that wake me up at night?

The swirling lights I can see that no one else can?

The line of people at my bedside in the middle of the night?

Are these things safe to say here?

I decided to take the risk, since I was not sleeping and I was basically a shell of a person anyway. What was the worst that could happen?

I opened my mouth and told her everything. Everything I'd never shared before. From the visits as a child to the hauntings as an adult. From the premonitions that all came true to the disembodied voices I sometimes heard.

These things I'd never had language for, just spewing out of me.

Pat listened, nodding. Chiming in every once in a while, with a "Mm-hmm. I've heard that before."

When I was finished recounting those experiences, Pat looked at me with a knowing.

"You, my dear, are a psychic medium," she told me matter-of-factly.

The way someone might say, "You, my dear, have brown hair."

As if this quality were just a normal character trait or physical characteristic.

As if waking up to the dead in your bedroom were as normal as waking up to your alarm. From there, she gently taught me how to have boundaries with spirit. Something I had never even considered from my hiding place under my covers.

Make the ghosts uncomfortable?

Ask for what I need?

No, thank you, I was content with just hiding and hoping they got the hint. Because, apparently, I am a people pleaser and a ghost pleaser.

But understanding I had a voice in the situation, some control over my ability, was a huge turning point. Except I had no interest in this life or in being a medium. So, after that session, I decided to shut it all down.

And it worked.

The nightly visitations stopped.

And so did the infections.

Overnight, they both vanished.

Spiritual Bypassing

For once, life felt pretty normal. But that feeling wouldn't last, because I had only put a Band-Aid on top of a big wound. After the miscarriage, this reservoir of rage that was filling inside me began spilling out, and the tools I had been using just weren't working, because I had been using the tools as a cover—ways to avoid, but not ways to heal. I was using them to stop the bleeding on pieces of myself I had severed. That pain, that hard stuff, was now oozing out, and I was being called to acknowledge it.

All of it.

You're probably familiar with positive affirmations and gratitude journaling. They are a big part of the self-help and spiritual world; maybe you've even used these tools yourself. If you are unfamiliar, positive affirmations are usually intentional statements we speak or write about to help reframe critical self-talk or boost confidence. And a gratitude journal is a log of things we are thankful for, helping to cultivate a mindset of appreciation.

I had used these tools for almost a decade. And at first, they really seemed to help me with reframing my fear-driven and very critical self-narrative. I would write myself encouraging notes and try to cancel out any negative thoughts I was having. Which, as someone with anxiety, often felt like a full-time job. For a while, this all helped.

But something was missing, and it became clear after the miscarriage.

Because, instead of allowing myself to feel the grief or the anger that was asking to be witnessed, I used gratitude journaling to squish those feelings down.

"*I'm so thankful for my health and that I have one healthy child*," I would write. Or, "*Thank you for this beautiful day.*" And let me be clear, there is nothing wrong with this practice. The problem for me at that time was, I wasn't feeling any of that. I was using these practices as a silver lining, a way to say, "*At least I still have . . .*" instead of sitting with my own pain.

And it started to feel like pushing a boulder uphill.

I didn't realize this at the time, but I was using these practices to bypass. Spiritual bypassing is a concept that was introduced in the 1980s by a psychologist named John Welwood. Welwood explains spiritual bypassing as the use of our spiritual practices or tools to avoid dealing with more difficult or unresolved emotions or issues. Oftentimes we don't even realize we are doing this, as it can be more of a coping mechanism in response to trauma or deeply uncomfortable emotions and feelings.

I found it easy to bypass because it *felt* like I was making progress even though I wasn't.

I just wanted to feel better, rather than to feel what I was feeling. I was bypassing and gaslighting myself and calling it ritual. I honestly thought this was the inner work. But healing and self-love wouldn't be found in repeating my affirmations and writing in my gratitude journal and calling that change.

It was going to be found unraveling my deepest, darkest corners and finding acceptance, knowing I am whole and complete not in spite of these parts but because of these parts. In letting my anger be seen and felt, in giving my grief space. It would be shining a light on my imperfections and knowing that I am worthy of being seen and loved.

Using Spiritual Tools Intentionally and Mindfully

The tools we all know and love, like gratitude journaling, positive affirmations, and even vision boarding, are often used to cultivate more peace, practice self-love, and draw forward positivity into our lives. There is absolutely nothing wrong with using these tools, and they can be beautiful and powerful practices to help shift our energy and our mindset. I still practice these today, just not as a cover-up.

It's not enough to simply repeat affirmations or write down things we're grateful for if we're ignoring the stuff underneath. Are we using affirmations to genuinely cultivate self-love and positive belief systems? Or are we merely looking for a silver lining and glossing over deeper fears, insecurities, and wounds that need to be witnessed? Gratitude journaling can be transformative when it comes from a place of authentic and genuine appreciation, and we're not using it to bypass or suppress the emotions that we have labeled negative or unworthy.

Affirmations can be a beautiful way to call in and highlight the things we want to feel, but they must be paired with an honest exploration of what's beneath. Are we using them to avoid feeling or witnessing the things we've labeled unworthy? And if you're reading this feeling really called out, please do not place judgment on yourself. I used my affirmations like this for years. I just wasn't aware I was doing it. No amount of bypassing will take us to the place of true healing. It's both sides: our shadow, our pain, our fears, along with our joys, our gratitude, our happiness, that invite us to see ourselves as whole.

The real magic happens when we use these tools *alongside* self-awareness and inner healing. With space to honor all the parts of ourselves: our shadow and light. We'll get more into this type of shadow work in Chapter 9.

The Invitation

It's hard to think of fear, anger, or pain as a friend inviting us in (those are some tough friends), but very often they are an invitation for deeper connection to ourselves—not a "negative" emotion to ignore. These emotions can show us where a boundary has been violated or where we are holding on to an insecurity or even just an old story.

We might receive many invitations to acknowledge these parts of ourselves, but they go unnoticed, or we ignore or numb them so we don't have to answer. Which makes a lot of sense, because it is no easy job to bring to the surface the darker parts of ourselves.

I believe a spiritual awakening is the organic unfolding that happens after you accept the invitation inward. Not a transcending of yourself and this world, but a deepening into yourself.

Answering the Call

I spent the better part of a decade silencing spirit and silencing my body. I think on some level a part of me knew that if I slowed down and listened, there would be an avalanche of suppressed stuff to deal with. It might mean witnessing emotions or patterns I wasn't ready to witness. It might mean coming face-to-face with the ways I was abandoning myself and hiding my pain. So I kept my fingers in my ears and hummed a metaphorical "La la la la la, I can't hear you!"

I wasn't ready.

And honestly, I don't think we can even hear the call until we are ready. And that's okay. Sometimes, we can't move deeper into the parts of ourselves until we've done some groundwork or until we've become so uncomfortable that it's the only option left. If we're not in a space where we can handle it, the call might feel terrifying. But when the time comes, everything will shift, and you will hear that call. You'll no longer need to avoid it, because deep down you know that answering is the only way forward, the path home to yourself.

I will never forget the night that spirit came back with one final invitation for me.

"She hears me! You hear me!"

I jolted awake.

A bright violet light was swirling to the left of me.

Not again.

The glee in her voice was palpable, though, causing me to smile.

"I can hear you," I replied, rubbing at my eyes.

"You have to do this."

It had been six years almost to the day since I had last been visited by spirit.

"Do what?" I asked.

"You already know."

And with that, she was gone.

My heart was racing, and yet I felt totally at peace, like I had been wrapped in the purest loving embrace, just like that figure that had appeared in my childhood room decades before.

Do what? I wondered as my mind began to take over. I could feel the weight of my husband sleeping next to me. I was always writing out goals for myself, and I had propped a little notecard on my nightstand with a list of what I wanted to achieve, like "write a book" and "be a yoga teacher."

Maybe she meant do those things? I thought as I glanced at it.

But in my heart, I knew.

It was time to answer the call, to let go of the grasp I had on the way I was living, and to surrender into all the unlit corners of myself. It was time to accept myself, embrace my abilities, and transform into what I knew was possible.

This was the start of the true healing journey.

What Are You Refusing to See?

Answering the call to step into our true selves is not easy, and it doesn't happen all at once. It's a journey of stops and starts, of unearthing the hidden pieces of ourselves and learning to integrate them into the whole of who we are. Facing the things we didn't want anyone else to know. The things we didn't even want ourselves to know. We start to shake out the patterns we've been following our whole lives, hanging them up to get a better look.

For me, that looked like accepting my mediumship abilities. But it was so much more than that. When I accepted this invitation to this part of myself, I was able to realize how much of myself I had been keeping hidden. My sensitive and introverted nature that I had been overriding. My hurt from feeling unseen and unheard as a child. My inability to express myself, acknowledge my emotions, or to ask for help. My nervous system that had been stuck in survival mode. These all rose to the surface, and I began to understand how I had been living under that cloak, performing for the world. And I was so tired of the act.

I invite you to do the same, to shine a light on the things you may have kept hidden. Not in a judgmental or self-shaming way, but with curiosity and tenderness.

✳ Questions for Reflection ✳

1. Is there a piece (or pieces) of yourself you have been refusing to acknowledge?

1. Probably, but I have no idea what they are.
2. I am avoiding most pieces of myself.
3. I know what parts of me want to be witnessed, but I'm struggling to make the move.
4. I express all areas of myself with ease.

What pieces of yourself are tugging on you to be seen? What fears come up as you think about making space for these pieces?

____

____

2. What practices or behaviors might you be using to bypass the difficult or uncomfortable emotions?

1. Basically all my practices are bypassing the difficult emotions.
2. I feel like I'm trying to face some of the harder stuff, but I think it's still very surface level.
3. I have begun to peel away at the edges and witness the more difficult emotions.
4. I have come face-to-face with my shadow.

3. How does your relationship with self-compassion appear when facing your shadow?

1. I struggle to offer myself compassion in difficult moments.
2. I can show myself kindness, but only for small challenges.
3. I'm learning to hold space for my darker emotions with tenderness.
4. I meet my shadow with compassion and curiosity.

I want you to keep this in mind as you are examining your spiritual practices: When it comes to spiritual bypassing, very often we might be bypassing something because we do not have the capacity to witness it yet. I think when we are ready to face our darker parts, we will know. The tricky part is when that doorbell rings and we *can* answer it, will we? Use this space below to reflect on any callings you've received to move inward and what answering them might feel like.

___

___

___

___

Accepting the Invitation

Answering the call to come home to ourselves is a sacred journey, a slow unraveling of the layers we've spent a lifetime weaving into place. It's not a one-and-done process; it is an ever-evolving path that we choose to walk. It requires us to look with compassion into ourselves. These hidden parts might bring discomfort, fear, and resistance, but they also hold the key for profound healing and growth. This process takes time, but each step, no matter how small, whether it's facing a buried part of ourselves with curiosity or having the courage to even answer the call, brings with it connection and healing.

As we answer the call to come home to ourselves, we will undoubtedly encounter old patterns and ways of moving. In the next chapter, we'll dive into the ties of perfectionism and people pleasing, structures we often build from a deep place of survival and a need to be accepted. We'll uncover how these behaviors, once intended to protect us, can actually become barriers to our authentic selves. We'll explore how these patterns intersect with our deep sensitivity and how in loosening their grip on us, we can move toward a deeper connection with ourselves and a sense of freedom. As you move through the next chapter, I encourage you to reflect on your own journey. Where have you traded self-trust for external guidance? What might become possible in embracing good enough and prioritizing yourself?

✳ 4 ✳

Permission Slips

The Patterns from Our Wounds

We all develop habits, or patterns, ones we subconsciously think are keeping us safe but end up being the things that are keeping us stuck. As I mentioned earlier, many of my patterns were really just the illusion of control. And when it came to my healing, I clung to that rigidity like a life raft. I believed my perfectionism and determination were my super strengths. But over time, I began to realize that they were just another cage. My relentless pursuit of healing, of bettering myself, the protocols I meticulously followed to "fix" myself, were counterproductive. They were leaving me disconnected from myself and keeping my nervous system in a frazzled state. But like anything else I discuss in this book, our patterns can also be invitations.

The Hidden Struggle of Controlling Everything

Does it often feel like you are performing? Like you are playing a part, being who and what you think is expected of you? Raise your hand if you have a very judgmental and critical inner voice. Do you have a hard time saying no or disappointing others and maybe the idea of any sort of conflict makes you want to throw up?

The exhaustion of striving for unattainable ideals and the relentless ache of prioritizing everyone but ourselves can be common for us highly sensitive women. Our deeper processing can be linked to a stronger reaction to criticism, a deeper sensitivity to rejection, and an intensity in social interactions. Our heightened empathy and attention to subtleties can become warped into patterns for self-abandonment. These patterns often stem from our childhoods and a deep desire to feel safe or a fear of rejection.

So many highly sensitive people are familiar with these behaviors because we are deep feelers, and as such we *deeply* feel the criticism and disapproval of others. In an effort to try and avoid this discomfort, we may have learned to do everything really, really well or to control things or to simply avoid conflict altogether. Essentially, they are our coping mechanisms.

But these behaviors are actually controlling.

For a long time, I labeled my attention to detail and ability to have everything in order all the time as a strength. Telling employers in job interviews, “Don’t worry; I always make sure it’s done perfectly,” hoping they would see that I was highly organized and determined, a hard worker who would always go above and beyond.

And while there are some positives to our perfectionist natures, like ambition and determination, there can be a really steep downside to living with extremely high standards for ourselves (and others). The energy it takes just trying to control everything is, in itself, exhausting. It is a restricting and constricting energy, not the expansive energy we all would prefer to be swimming in.

Restricting

The idea of restricting ourselves is like putting constraints (either knowingly or unknowingly) that limit our actions and choices, often out of a need to control a situation or to avoid failure. Incredibly high expectations of ourselves and a tendency to overachieve at everything in life is not really a sustainable way to live and can result in anxiety, stress, and an overall burden on our mental and physical well-being.

I know, because I've created a lot of weird and strict rules for myself throughout my life. None that I've written down in a secret "rules handbook," just ones I've sort of abided to or else I would consider myself a failure.

For example, before I was able to embrace my curly hair, I refused to be seen in public if my hair wasn't in a perfect bouncy blowout. A run to the grocery store required this pageantry-level hair. No exceptions, literally. Outside of my family, most people didn't know I had curly hair. I forced myself to finish any book that I had picked up to read, even if it was insufferable. When I began a strict fitness regimen, I pushed myself to work out seven days a week, with no rest days or days off, even when I was sick.

My strict guidelines didn't stop with myself either. The high expectations I had would often spill over onto others in my life. For example, when my husband took up running, he had been on a running streak, going out every morning to get in his steps. Then one morning he didn't run. And then afternoon came and went. Then the evening, and *I* was getting nervous. I asked him if it bothered him to break his streak. To which he replied, in his relaxed way, not at all, he was taking a day off. I was literally sweating. "But if you miss a day, it's like your running streak won't even count," I declared.

These were the sort of rules I had created for myself, and my gosh, were they restricting and exhausting. I didn't know it at the time, but there was a label for my behavior. I was a perfectionist. I used to understand this label to mean someone who was really good at what they did, but it wasn't until this intense perfectionism started showing up in my journey to heal my infections that I began to see how detrimental it actually was.

Perfectionism

Perfectionism is characterized by having incredibly high standards for ourselves and is often accompanied by a strong, critical inner voice. The deep fear of failure can lead to anxiety, depression, or intense stress. Perfectionism can manifest in all areas of our lives, from work to relationships to personal achievements, and it can be deeply rooted in shame and the feeling of not being good enough.

As children, we may have felt that nothing we did was enough or that we had to prove ourselves over and over in order to gain love. So we developed these habits of doing more, and being the best, to protect ourselves and to stay safe, loved, and above all, connected to our caregivers. That connection was our safety.

As I mentioned, highly sensitive people are deeply attuned to the emotions and reactions of those around us. As children, this was true of our caregivers. Many of us heard things like we're "too sensitive" or "too dramatic" or [insert any version of this from your own childhood]. We may have developed a hyper-awareness of how we were being perceived by others. This led us to feel like we needed to change ourselves or go above and beyond to make up for this perceived "flaw" of sensitivity, which we'll get into in the next chapter, Healing the Sensitivity Wound. Over time, we developed these unrealistic expectations of ourselves in order to gain approval and protect ourselves from criticism or rejection. We ended up commissioning our worth from others and constantly performing.

I want to share with you how this pattern emerged in my attempt to cure my physical health issues.

Perfectionism in Healing

If you've ever tried to heal physical symptoms, you know there can be an overwhelming amount of information, especially with access to everything on the Internet. The health-and-wellness industry is a billion-dollar industry that often lacks regulations and can be intensely competitive in terms of getting our attention. It is imperative on your own healing journey that you recognize this in order to make informed decisions around your own care.

One expert suggests this method; another expert debunks that method and offers their own. Doctors tell you one thing; practitioners tell you another. The Internet tells you your headache is cancer. It can be really hard to know where to focus when all you want to do is feel better. This is where our own inner wisdom can be a guiding force, but we'll get more into that in Chapter 7.

As my own recurring infections persisted through any kind of conventional medical treatment, I began to search outside the box for ways to heal myself. I tried things like:

Giving up sugar
Giving up alcohol
Giving up caffeine
Giving up gluten
Giving up corn
Giving up dairy
Giving up processed foods
Not mixing nuts and berries
Not eating until 10 A.M.
Not eating after 10 P.M.
Starting my day with a shot of apple cider vinegar
Endless blood tests and labs
Stool tests
Candida tests
Allergy tests
Ultrasounds
Anatomy scans
Thyroid testing
Growing my own cultures to make probiotics
Drinking one beer every morning on an empty stomach (This is a good story for another day!)
Mixing gag-worthy concoctions of herbs
Oil pulling
Juicing fresh celery juice every morning
Foot baths
All the supplements
Giving up fragrances and scented soaps
Using baking soda in place of shampoo . . . and so on.

I spent thousands upon thousands of dollars on doctors' visits, prescription medications, over-the-counter treatments, protocols, supplements, and more. Like a tried-and-true perfectionist, I focused with *precision* on all the right steps. I checked the boxes; I followed the orders to facilitate my healing.

And then, just as when anything goes wrong for a perfectionist, when I had a flare-up, I felt like a giant failure.

What had I done wrong?

Maybe it was the dairy; I shouldn't have eaten that ice cream. Or what if it was the corn? Corn is riddled with GMOs. I knew I shouldn't have had that taco.

It's probably because I allowed myself that piece of cake on my birthday.

So, I restricted, and I restricted, and I was, as my husband likes to say, "thoroughly unrelaxed."

At the height of trying to control my symptoms, we had planned a little family vacation away to the beach; our first vacation in *years*. I was packing up the standard family items: bathing suits, diapers, pajamas, all the essentials. But when it came time to pack for myself, I was completely overwhelmed.

How am I going to do this?

What am I going to eat while we're there?

Is there room to pack my juicer?

At this point, I had cut out most enjoyable foods. I was juicing fresh celery every morning. I was choking down supplements three times a day. I was mixing tinctures like a mad scientist and gagging them down.

Now, I am all for eating whole foods and taking care of ourselves. But, I had become so afraid of and hypervigilant of ingredients, labels, and foods that the stress from that was no doubt adding to my health issues. I was trying so hard to control my health and force healing, and I was more stressed than I could ever remember being.

Standing in the kitchen of our vacation rental, holding my juicer with tears streaming down my face, I said to my husband, "I can't remember the last time I actually felt relaxed."

And, even worse? Healing was nowhere in sight. The symptoms were raging on. In fact, in my suitcase was another prescription to treat another infection.

As I wept in the kitchen, trying to find a spot for my juicer, I realized that I might have chronic infections, but I was also chronically stressed, operating from pure survival mode, and it became clear if I couldn't find a way to relax, I was never going to heal.

It wasn't the corn that was making me sick.

It was the stress.

It was the pressure I had been placing on myself; it was the fear I was deeply holding on to. The secret I was keeping about my mediumship. The boundaries I didn't know how to express and the standards I was holding myself to with zero flexibility. Something needed to change.

People Pleasing

Just as our perfectionism can stem from an intense desire to avoid failure or criticism and to protect ourselves, our tendency to people-please can also be a built-in safety mechanism and fear of judgment, especially when we're so attuned to the emotions and reactions of those around us. This drive to prioritize others can lead us to suppress our own needs in favor of maintaining the relationship, even at the cost of ourselves.

Being labeled as "too sensitive" or "too much" can make us feel like we need to shrink ourselves or seek permission to take up space and fully exist as we are. As perfectionists, we hate the idea of making mistakes, but we also hate, maybe even more so, the idea of letting people down. We're more than willing to make ourselves uncomfortable for the chance to keep everyone else comfortable.

Have you ever been asked, at the last minute, to bake 24 cupcakes for your kids' class, or maybe your boss tells you at 5 P.M. on the way out the door that you need to write that report for tomorrow? The voice inside you says, "I don't have the capacity for this," but you end up saying, "Sure! No problem!" It's hard to express our needs or listen to ourselves when we've spent a lifetime prioritizing others and keeping the peace.

This doesn't mean we never say yes to things we don't feel like doing; unfortunately, that's a part of life. But the shift happens when we acknowledge that voice telling us, *I don't have the capacity for this*, letting it be heard, and honoring it in other ways when saying no isn't an option.

I would avoid conflict at all costs.

If I ever tried to set a boundary, or even just share my opinion on a controversial topic, my voice would shake, my skin would flush pink, and usually my eyes would swell with tears. I did not know how to use my voice, because I had never really had the opportunity to safely do so. And after a lifetime of prioritizing others, I definitely didn't know how to choose myself, or to prioritize my comfort, if it meant someone would so much as glance at me the wrong way.

Maybe you relate? There was a time that I thought this was a giant weakness, a flaw that made me "less than." But I can now see little Danica trying so hard to share her voice or be as brave as the extroverted kids, when she was just built different, and she needed a different support that wasn't available to her. I now see how prioritizing others and shrinking herself became her means of safety.

Recognizing how deeply rooted our patterns of perfectionism and people pleasing can be, it becomes clear that in order to begin to free ourselves from these patterns, we must first give ourselves permission.

Permission Slips

As a society, we are conditioned to believe that our worth comes from our productivity, and our productivity must "exceed expectations" for it to be considered mildly good enough. I'm actually pretty sure that's the rating system used across school systems and corporate America.

From the time we're school aged, someone else assigns our worth through report cards and then later through college acceptance letters and then performance reviews and pay grades.

These systems, this outsourcing of our worth, chisel away at our inner foundation of intuitive knowing and inherent value. I felt this firsthand when leaving the corporate environment for stay-at-home motherhood. I could feel my value and worth draining from me. The labels, the letters behind my name, the things I had built around myself to *prove* to the world, to prove to myself, that I was valuable, smart, and important dribbled away until they were gone.

I desperately wanted (maybe even needed) to be seen, and now there I was, in the most invisible role, feeling very much unseen but still trying to do it perfectly in the hopes that that would define my value.

As I peeled myself away from corporate life, I saw how the stress and busyness had been a distraction that kept me focused outside of myself—a pattern I had been following from childhood. The disconnection was becoming intolerable.

The permission I was seeking needed to come from within, but I had been avoiding "within" like the plague. Sitting still was uncomfortable, and also wildly unproductive, so it wasn't really top of list for me at the time. I would come to realize that this stillness, this inward exploration, was the only medicine I truly needed. It was in stillness that I would begin to understand the coping mechanisms I had built for myself: the perfectionism, the people pleasing, the prioritizing everyone else—these were all results of the four core wounds we will discuss in the next part of the book. And once I had an awareness of these, I began to heal them with a whole lot of self-compassion and by taking actions I normally wouldn't, like saying no. This was a muscle I developed over time, and as I did, I found myself more and more comfortable with giving myself the permission I needed.

I was so focused on the external, on who had the answers to save me, that I never stopped to wonder if I held the key the whole time.

At some point, we have to see our worth and give ourselves permission. Whether it's permission to mess up, to follow a dream, to leave an unsupportive relationship, or simply to choose ourselves. Because no one is going to give us that permission. There is no authority outside of ourselves that can give this permission to us. But I'm not sure it's as easy as telling ourselves we are allowed and then just going and doing it. If we don't feel safe in our own bodies, it can feel almost impossible to step out of this restrictive box we've built for ourselves.

Am I even allowed to be doing this?

It's a question I asked myself several times a day when I set out as an entrepreneur, to post online, to host a workshop, to write a book—whatever it was. I was waiting for the permission police to pop out and stop me. They never did, and over time I realized they don't exist. They don't exist for you either. You are allowed to show up, to be seen, to use your voice, to take up space, to follow your dreams, and to try.

Applying Self-Compassion in Your Own Life

If you have been reading along and are noticing that perhaps you also have some patterns of perfectionism and people pleasing, that's okay! As we embark on healing some of the wounds we've been carrying, the first thing to call forward is gentle self-compassion. Healing can feel hard, and without this grace and compassion for ourselves, it is only going to feel harder.

Take notice of what comes up when you think about showing yourself compassion. Does it feel weird or uncomfortable? Does it stir up guilt or make you roll your eyes? For many of us, compassion can feel uncomfortable, foreign even, especially when we've spent so much of our lives with a critical inner voice, being hard on ourselves, or pushing ourselves to "do more" to prove our worth.

As with any of this healing work, the first step is awareness. Start by noticing how you talk to yourself throughout the day. Are you highly critical of yourself when you mess up (or even when you succeed)? Do you constantly strive to be perfect or keep moving the bar for yourself? Maybe you ignore the small wins because they never feel like enough. Recognizing those patterns is the key.

Before we move on to the next part of this book, try this process to help you gently shift into a space of self-compassion:

1. **Check in with your expectations.**

   What are your expectations for yourself right now, and are they realistic? Do they feel restrictive or expansive? Perfectionism has a way of making everything feel like a pass/fail test that's rigged so we always fail. But *good enough* is really all there is. If you find yourself obsessing over a practice, or getting stuck, remind yourself there is no right or wrong way.

2. **Tend to your inner child.**

   Think about the little version of you, the one who might have been told they weren't good enough or who felt unseen. Little you deserves your love and care. How can you nurture that part of yourself as you move forward? Make space for her and let her know she's loved just as she is.

3. **Find stillness.**

   Find stillness to explore some of what's under the surface, calling to be witnessed. Taking time to sit quietly is an act of self-compassion in itself. In this stillness, you create space to connect with your body and mind, to notice what's there. This might be uncomfortable at first, but I promise, the more you sit with it and simply allow what's there to be seen, the more space you make to shift.

4. **Laugh and have fun.**

   Play is an antidote to perfectionism. If you make a mistake, try making it silly. Respond with something lighthearted like "now that I've got your attention. . . ." Laughter and joy help to loosen the grip of that critical inner voice that tells us we're not enough. Make time for the things that make you smile, because those moments are part of the healing.

5. **Above all, give yourself permission.**

   The most important thing you can do is to *give yourself permission*. Permission to be imperfect, permission to try and fail, permission to just be. Create a mantra for yourself like "I am allowed to try."

Choosing to show ourselves a bit more compassion can have such a huge impact on our daily life as well as our nervous system and healing. Be patient and gentle with yourself as you start to shift these old habits. It's okay if it feels difficult or unfamiliar at first; healing often happens in these in-between spaces, in the uncertainty and transitions.

✳ Questions for Reflection ✳

1. Where does your sense of worth come from?

1. I need external validation to feel valuable.
2. On some levels I know I am enough, but it's shaky, and I often lean on others for a dose of validation.
3. I feel a steady sense of value not usually tied to my achievements.
4. I know I am inherently worthy.

What stories from your past might be dictating your worth? Make some space for them here. You don't have to change them or rewrite them, just begin to take notice.

____

____

2. Does it feel like you always need to be in control?

1. I am a certified control freak.
2. I like to be in control but am able to ease up sometimes.

3. I am pretty good at balancing what is in my control and what is out of my control.
4. I am a go-with-the-flow girl.

3. How do you handle your mistakes or perceived imperfections?

1. A mistake or imperfection can unravel my whole day.
2. I feel overwhelmed when I make a mistake, but I try to learn from it.
3. I accept my mistakes as part of my journey and treat myself with compassion.
4. I embrace my imperfections and see them as opportunities to grow.

How would it feel to stop forcing and instead make space for allowing, and how can you release control a bit?

____

____

If you checked off mostly 1's or 2's, can you begin to reflect on why that might be? Use the space below to journal how you might begin to embrace your imperfect and authentic self.

____

____

Key Takeaways

We all have patterns and beliefs we've developed along the way, and the patterns of perfectionism and people pleasing can be deeply ingrained in our lives as women and highly sensitive folks. As you reflect on this chapter, remember that these behaviors were adapted as a way to survive, and there is something beautiful about that. We wanted to feel safe and loved, and we deserved that; we still deserve that. These are not our flaws; they were simply our attempts to meet the expectations of others and stay connected. But, as we learn to unravel these layers, we begin to see that they are not who we are. By giving ourselves compassion and permission to step outside the rigid structures, we can make space for our own healing and find a path that is more aligned with our truth and our soul.

In Reflection

We looked at how awakening often begins when we're pulled into our depths and faced with change. This is often caused by a catalyst, an event that shakes the very foundation of our lives, or at the very least highlights that that foundation was shaky to begin with. It upends everything we thought we knew. We start to question how we're living, who we really are, and what we truly want. In these moments, we are often faced with a choice: to answer the call or to ignore it.

Answering the call is rarely the easier path, but it leads to a truer, more aligned life if we choose to follow it. It requires us to face ourselves, confront the patterns that have been driving our lives, and begin to choose a different way. It means remembering our worth, reclaiming our voice, taking back our power, and moving through the world with intention.

As we conclude the first part of this book, I invite you to pause and reflect on your own journey thus far. In what ways have you been called to question the path you've been walking? Have you been ignoring the call? Reflect on the moments that have sparked change for you. How did you handle them?

Take a moment to honor where you are in your own journey and recognize the courage it takes to even ask these questions. The path ahead may not always be clear, but as you move inward, this connection will lead to a deeper trust in yourself.

What Lies Ahead

As we journey into the next part of this book, we will explore some of the common wounds that stand in the way of our true connection to ourselves and our ability to honor our truth. These wounds, rooted in past experiences, cultural conditioning, and societal pressures, have shaped how we move through the world and relate to our own sensitivity, body, mind, spirit, and divinity. In the coming chapters, we will dive into the healing of these core wounds, beginning with the Sensitivity Wound, where you'll discover that you are not "too sensitive," as you've probably been told, but that your sensitivity is a powerful gift. We'll then explore the Connection Wound, learning how to move out of autopilot and reconnect with mind, body, and spirit in a way that honors us. Followed by the Body Wound, which will invite you to reconnect with the deep wisdom of your body. We'll end Part II by exploring the Witch Wound, a wound that affects us all, and you'll discover how to reclaim your true divine power.

Each chapter offers gentle tools, reflections, and practices for healing and transformation. As always, listen to yourself and move gently through this next part. You know your truth best; take what speaks to you and leave the rest.

PART II

THE FOUR CORE WOUNDS

As we embark on Part II of the book, we'll begin to explore a bit deeper, dipping into some tender spaces where old wounds live. These are the wounds that may have told you that you were too sensitive, kept you disconnected from your body, made you fearful of your own power, or had you questioning yourself and your inner guidance. While these may have helped shape you, becoming aware of them and reclaiming choice is how you reclaim your power. These are not meant to be diagnoses or to pathologize your experiences, but to help you make sense of them.

As you read through these next chapters, keep in mind that many of these wounds have been passed down through family lines, culture, society, and even collective trauma. The wound did not start with you, but the healing can.

Remember to hold and practice that compassion for yourself as you move through this section, and always follow your own lead. Let your body, your own inner wisdom, and your capacity be your guide while understanding that sometimes the things we feel the most resistance toward can be a signal to where the most healing needs to happen.

This part of the book explores the four core wounds that I believe many sensitive women carry:

- **The Sensitivity Wound**—the belief that your sensitivity is a design flaw, something to "fix"
- **The Connection Wound**—feeling disconnected from your body, spirit, or self and the weaponization of fear
- **The Body Wound**—the mistrust and disconnection from your physical body
- **The Witch Wound**—the fear of your own power, magic, and voice

Each chapter will offer research, reflection, personal stories, insights, and gentle practices to help you begin the process of reclaiming what has always been yours: your wholeness, your wisdom, and your power.

Let's begin.

✶ 5 ✶

Healing the Sensitivity Wound

You Are Not Too Sensitive

I know you help the earthworm back to the
soil after it's rained.

I know you hide your tears when passing a freshly
chopped tree.

I know you apologize to the flower when you've
stepped on it.

I know you collect the spider lost in your home
and place her back outside.

I know you brake for the squirrels and pick up
garbage off the beach.

I know you smile at strangers even when you're
breaking inside.

And I know your kindness has been taken advantage of and
your heart swells with grief that isn't even yours to carry.

I know you feel so out of place and often out of hope.

And I know it all feels pointless in a world
intent on destruction.

But it matters.

And you matter.

You aren't out of place; you are here to
change everything.

Odds are, if you picked up this book, you're probably a fairly sensitive person. I look at the term *sensitive* as an umbrella term that can refer to different kinds of sensitivity—such as emotional sensitivity, sensory sensitivity (how strongly you perceive sights, sounds, or smells), or physical sensitivity, like your tolerance for pain. Or maybe the lesser-known sensitivity to energy, which is the ability to perceive subtle energetic fields, different vibrational frequencies, or even spiritual energies. Perhaps you are sensitive to all of the above. I know I am.

One of my strongest psychic abilities is sensing energy—individual and collective. I can feel it in my body, deeply. It's one of the gifts I use most when I have a session with a client. I can feel what they are feeling, emotionally and physically. It allows me to tap into what is going on in their lives, in their bodies, and even tune in to early experiences.

It's also the ability I use when I am connecting with a client's loved one who has crossed over. If that loved one passed of a heart attack, I might feel pain in my chest. I once had a client whose deceased mother was present in the session, and as soon as I connected to her energy, I was struggling to breathe. It was so intense that I had to pause the session to be able to get some air. As it turned out, her mother had passed from lung cancer, and at the end of her life, she severely struggled to breathe at all. I often feel a sense of breathlessness when the loved one has passed from a lung-related issue, or I will feel dizzy if they passed from a fall. It took some practice, but these subtle energies are simply clues into a vast world we cannot always see.

My whole life, no matter what someone was doing or saying, it was as if I could look right into their energy and see the truth. I could see and feel their pain, their sadness, their anger. As you can imagine, before I realized I had this ability, it could be quite overwhelming to be around people. I had no understanding of what was happening to me physically, emotionally, or energetically. Maybe you have had a similar experience with feeling and sensing energy but have never understood it as a gift. My aim is to show you that it is definitely a gift.

Let's first look at different types of sensitivities.

Types of Sensitive Individuals

As mentioned, there are several variations and ways in which our sensitivity can manifest. Whether it's emotional, physical, or energetic, it will likely look slightly different for each of us. Let's start by looking at what it means to be a highly sensitive person (HSP), and then we'll explore what an empath is. I will include introversion as well, which is technically not a sensitivity but more a social orientation, although introverts can have many overlapping qualities with both HSPs and empaths, so it's worth a mention.

These are not meant to be labels to live by, but merely to help you understand yourself and how you operate a bit better.

The Highly Sensitive Person (HSP)

A highly sensitive person (HSP) refers to a neurological trait that involves deep processing, meaning an HSP has a more finely tuned nervous system than the average person, making them sensitive to physical, emotional, sensory, and social stimuli. HSPs are deep processors and take in the world around them on a deep level.

Key traits include:

- A strong sense of empathy and emotional responsiveness. HSPs experience emotions more intensely than others (both their own emotions and the emotions of others)
- A deep processing of information and experiences. HSPs can be very observant, noticing details and even shifts in facial expressions that others tend to miss
- Can be easily overstimulated by sensory input, such as noise, lights, crowds, or smells
- A heightened awareness of subtleties in their environment. HSPs can feel a shift in energy in the environment (like if you've ever walked into a room after an argument and could feel the tension)
- A strong connection to intuition and often a need for solitude to recharge their energy
- Difficulty watching anything gory, violent, or overly negative or sad

According to research, highly sensitive people make up about 15 to 20 percent of the population. Within this highly sensitive group is a subgroup known as empaths.

The Empath

Empath is not a clinically recognized term or a diagnosis, but talk to any empath and they know what they feel. An empath is described as someone who not only understands the emotions of others but actually *feels* them as if they were their own. This is different from the regular empathy that most humans experience. Having empathy is understanding what someone else is feeling. Being an empath is actually feeling what they are feeling. Empaths are highly attuned to the emotional states of others and can have a difficult time differentiating between what is theirs and what is someone else's. Because being an empath is not a clinical diagnosis, there is not an official tally, but researchers estimate that about 1 to 2 percent of the population are considered to be empaths.

Key traits include:

- A deep emotional connection with others
- The ability to sense subtle emotional shifts and unspoken feelings
- Difficulty distinguishing their own emotions from those of others
- The ability to not only feel others' emotions, but sometimes others' physical pain, sensations, or symptoms in their own bodies
- A strong connection to intuition and a need for solitude to recharge their energy
- Difficulty watching anything gory or violent, or overly negative or sad
- Usually quite connected spiritually, having had experiences of seeing or hearing passed loved ones or spiritual beings

I will get further into what it means to be an empath later in this chapter, as there are many interesting experiences that define this ability. Whether you are a highly sensitive person, an empath, or both, you might also consider yourself an introvert, which shares some overlapping characteristics with being highly sensitive.

The Introvert

Introverts are people who are most comfortable in low-stimulation environments or alone rather than in large social gatherings. Introversion isn't considered a form of sensitivity, but it overlaps with many traits of high sensitivity. And since research shows that about 70 percent of HSPs are introverts, the connection is worth noting.

Key traits include:

- A preference for quiet or solitary activities
- Can become drained by prolonged social interaction
- A need for time alone to recharge their energy
- Reflective and requires time to think before speaking
- Often creative and imaginative
- A heightened sensitivity to dopamine and therefore find pleasure in gentle and solo activities
- Can become overstimulated by too much sensory input

As you can see, these three categories have many overlapping traits. A person can be an HSP, an empath, and an introvert simultaneously, or any combination of the three. These distinctions are not meant to be boxes that define us, but they can help us better navigate our own experiences and needs. For the purpose of this chapter, we are going to be focusing on the experiences of being an empath.

It Starts with Awareness

Perhaps you become very overwhelmed in crowded places or loud gatherings. Or you can physically feel a buzzing or vibrating energy under your skin in those crowded places. Maybe you've had an experience where your friend had a headache, and then all of a sudden you also had a headache. Or you just started crying when in a group setting and had literally no clue why or what was happening. Or you walked into a room and were overcome with tension or fear. Or you became incredibly drained around certain people, as if your battery just completely ran out. Maybe you're deeply connected to Mother Earth and you can feel her pain, or feel the trees breathe.

You're not crazy. And you're definitely not alone. These are common experiences for the empath.

These exact scenarios had played out over and over in my life, but I never knew why or even considered that not everyone was experiencing the world in this way.

I vividly remember the first time I had an outside-looking-in awareness of it, like I was watching it take place. It was a clear, blue October day, and we were walking through the streets of Seoul. I was having a great time taking in the sights, history, and culture. I popped into a shop to browse and was greeted by two women who worked there. The shop was otherwise empty. After looking around briefly, I thanked the women and made my way back into the crowded street.

My husband was waiting for me, and as I happily crossed the street toward him, I was suddenly overcome with extreme sadness, so much so that I involuntarily began sobbing. It felt like I had stepped into a dark cloud, overtaken by intense grief. My husband, alarmed, began asking, "What's wrong? What happened?"

"I don't know," I replied.

It was a familiar answer to the question, "Why are you crying?"—a question I seemed to be asked frequently throughout my life while sobbing in crowded places. As a highly sensitive person, or empath, perhaps you recognize this scenario from your own life.

The answer "I don't know" was the truth. I didn't understand why I was crying; I was having a great day. These feelings of immense grief and sadness that hit me like a wave were not mine. For the first time, I distinctly made the correlation that what I was feeling had nothing to do with me.

I had unintentionally taken on the emotions of someone nearby.

So, What Is an Empath?

Empaths are highly attuned to the emotions, feelings, and energy of others and often experience these as if they are their own. Empaths are also known for being great listeners and space holders. They are naturally intuitive and just seem to know not only how you're feeling, but deeper information as well.

While these might sound like generally positive traits, being highly empathic and attuned to others can come with its set of challenges, especially if we are not empowered to understand or honor our sensitivity. Let's discuss some of the underlying challenges of being an empath.

The Power of Feeling Deeply

As highly sensitive folks, we process our world on a deeper level than most. Sounds, smells, lights, energy, emotions—these all land in our bodies in a more profound and intense way.

All humans have an energy field that extends outward into their environment. I like to think of us highly sensitives as having invisible energy tentacles (almost like an octopus) that extend further out into our environment than most people, sensing and collecting information.

Do you remember those plasma balls in all the science stores in the 1980s and '90s? If you're too young, these plasma balls were clear glass globes with an electrode in the center and filled with gasses that, when energized, would create colorful tendrils of light, like tentacles. When you touched the glass with your finger, the tendrils would intensify and follow your hand. Picture an empath's energy tendrils kind of like this. They extend into the environment and react to different energy, almost drawing that energy (or those emotions/feelings/sensations) back into their own bodies.

As empaths, I see us as having more energy tentacles and a farther reach than the average person. This is a beautiful thing, as it allows us to pick up on the subtle energy changes that most people miss. It allows us to connect deeply with others and empathize with what they feel, because we can feel it as our own. And it allows us to take in our world in a beautifully deep way: Sunsets might bring us to tears, the laughter of children might fill us with warmth, and even the smallest of moments can be deeply meaningful. Experiencing life so deeply can be beautiful, but it can also bring on its own set of challenges.

As empaths, we might be prone to emotional overwhelm due to our ability to absorb or take on others' feelings. It can sometimes be difficult to separate what feelings are our own and what feelings belong to someone close to us—or even a stranger. We are incredibly sensitive to our environment, and crowded or overly loud spaces tend to overstimulate and drain us.

Because of our heightened awareness and sensitivity to others' emotions, it's not unusual for us to develop people-pleasing tendencies. When we are feeling someone's disappointment as our own, it makes sense that, in order to avoid that discomfort in ourselves, we would prioritize others. Similarly, perfectionism can emerge from a fear of failure or a need for approval, especially to sidestep criticism that we experience with amplified intensity.

Feeling misunderstood is a common emotional experience among empaths. And it makes sense that most people cannot fully grasp what it feels like navigating a world that often feels too loud and too intense, and they are often dismissive of our sensitivity in general, as only an estimated 2 percent of the population are wired this way. We've all had the experience of being called "too sensitive" or "so dramatic" or told that we "need thicker skin" in a society that mistakes our depth for a design flaw or a weakness. These labels, while they are probably not intended to be malicious or hurtful, over time, teach us to dismiss our sensitive and intuitive side, silence our emotions, and even apologize for existing as we are. These tiny erasures of self can leave us questioning whether our ability to feel deeply is actually a gift or just a burden we must quietly bear.

On top of that, as deep feelers who are intimately aware of others' emotions, we might find ourselves mistaking this awareness for a responsibility to fix them. Our awareness and ability to feel what others carry does not equal a responsibility to fix. Read that again. Our awareness of and ability to feel does not mean we are responsible for others. This is a common experience for empaths, often because we believe, on a deep, unconscious level, that our worth is measured by our ability to fix, soothe, or even heal others.

Are Empaths Born or Made?

All humans have the capacity to feel empathy, but how did 2 percent of the population get their highly empathic abilities? Are we born empaths, or are we shaped by our childhood experiences? The answer, according to research, is both.

I have my own theory about this, but let's start with the science. Some studies suggest that high empathy does have a biological origin. Look at the mirror neuron system (MNS), a system of specialized neurons located in specific regions of the brain. The MNS activates when we are performing an action or when we are observing others, and it enables us to learn or imitate. The MNS also plays a critical role in empathy by allowing us to read facial expressions, understand emotions, and even learn others' intentions by allowing neural mirroring of observed actions and emotional states. The most obvious examples of how the MNS works is when we see someone get hurt. We flinch when we observe someone else scrape their knee or get hit by a ball, as if we are experiencing the pain in our own bodies.

Studies suggest that the mirror neuron system is more active, or heightened, in empaths or people who are highly sensitive. According to Dr. Judith Orloff, a psychiatrist and author who specializes in treating highly sensitive people and empaths, empaths have a hyper-responsive mirror neuron system. This extra activity in our brains links to feeling others' emotions more intensely. In other words, your brain doesn't just recognize emotions on someone's face; it also helps you physically feel what they're feeling, which is why empathy can feel so automatic and powerful. One way Dr. Orloff has described this ability is as mirror-touch synesthesia. Synesthesia, if you're unfamiliar, is a rare neurological condition in which two senses are paired in the brain, for example, when someone can see music as colors or taste words. You can think of the ability of an empath in this same way; with mirror-touch synesthesia, as Dr. Orloff describes, empaths can feel the emotions and sensations of other people in their own bodies.

But the genetic predisposition to being highly sensitive and empathic is often not the whole story. There is a significant body of psychological research that points to childhood trauma and adverse experiences as having an impact on the formation of these empathic traits. Children who grow up in emotionally abusive, unpredictable, chaotic, or neglectful environments often develop hypervigilance, a trauma-informed survival mechanism. Hypervigilance manifests as a constant scanning of facial expressions, vocal tones, emotional shifts, and environment to predict danger and mitigate harm.

When we look at the shaping of high sensitivity from this perspective, it becomes clear that children can learn to feel deeply and sense shifts in their caregivers in order to respond quickly to protect themselves. Over time, this adaptation can lead to chronic stress, emotional exhaustion, and difficulty distinguishing genuine threats from neutral stimuli in safer environments. We will get more into the impact of childhood adverse experiences in Chapter 7, but this is where we can see a connection between empaths and trauma. Though I will state that not all empathy is a trauma response.

Empaths and Codependency

This early conditioning to be attuned to the needs and emotions of others can set the stage for a lifetime of blurred or confusing boundaries. Many empaths grow up equating their value with their ability to manage the emotional landscapes around them. They become the peacekeepers and the mediators, overriding their own needs to try and stay safe. Over time, this can morph into a deeper issue: *codependency*.

Codependency is characterized as a condition, or relationship dynamic, where an individual can become reliant on another person, often neglecting their own needs in order to "help" or fix someone else. It is not classified as a psychological diagnosis, but more a recognized behavior that can become unhealthy. Codependent individuals often have low self-esteem and a strong need for approval. They struggle with boundaries and expressing their own needs and have a tendency toward caretaking in a relationship. At its core, it's not a disease or pathology but a learned behavior in seeking love, safety, or worth through another person.

In Melody Beattie's book *Codependent No More*, she discusses how these patterns in codependency are often learned in childhood, especially in homes where love was conditional or emotional chaos was the norm. In these environments, children may internalize the belief that they must earn love through service, sacrifice, or emotional labor. For empaths, this can become a catch-22: our greatest gift, our sensitivity, becomes tangled in a survival pattern that makes it hard to know where we end and others begin. Codependents tend to prioritize others' needs and seek validation by taking care of others. This behavior is often deeply rooted in a lack of self-worth or self-love stemming from childhood, where we grew up in dysfunction or love was conditional.

Here are some common traits of codependency:

- Prioritizing others above yourself, often neglecting yourself altogether
- Needing the approval and validation of others
- Low self-esteem and low self-worth (needing external approval to raise both)
- Sacrificing yourself, your needs, or your goals in support of the relationship
- Feeling responsible for others' emotional states
- Feeling responsible for others' actions
- Feeling the need to manage or control others, or become overinvolved in their lives
- Unable to express your opinion, especially if it's "negative"
- Unable to engage in healthy conflict
- Avoiding conflict altogether
- Difficulty setting boundaries
- A fear of abandonment

Codependent empaths often absorb others' emotions as their own and will prioritize others' needs, leading to imbalances in relationships. We feel responsible for others' feelings and happiness, usually with a complete disregard for our own. This only adds to our hypervigilance and constant need to manage the emotions and feelings around us. It's important to note that, while empaths might be prone to emotional absorption and blurred boundaries, that in no way means that all empaths become codependent.

For most of my life, I didn't realize I was an empath. I knew I had anxiety; I knew I was extremely sensitive to others' emotions, but I didn't realize how I was absorbing and storing so much of what wasn't mine to carry, and I had been doing it for a lifetime.

When my husband would have a stressful day at work, I could feel his energy right away. I would scan his facial expressions and immediately become tense, asking him what was wrong. When he would answer nothing, I would grasp harder, dig deeper, asking, Did something happen? Was he angry? Was he sad? And finally, was he mad at me? I could not relax until I had found the root cause and fixed it. I needed to know it wasn't my fault, but I also needed to make it better, often abandoning myself completely in order to do so. His stressful day became my stressful day. I couldn't separate the two. And my husband is the safest person I know. It was a learned behavior because my energy had always belonged to everyone around me, and it was exhausting.

The coping mechanisms I developed began to feel like I was drowning from within. When I started to become aware of these patterns, I wanted out. The cost of keeping others comfortable at my own expense was becoming too high. I needed to find a solid ground to stand on. I needed to find myself again.

The Cultural Narrative and Learning to Cope

Whether your sensitivity was born out of survival, or is simply in your genes, one thing is true: We live in a sensitive-averse culture. We center productivity, overriding our bodies, toughness (physical and emotional), and the ability to push through and persevere over any kind of emotional depth, empathy, slowness, or gentleness. We hear phrases like "Toughen up" and "You're fine!" when we cry or show emotion. Through repeated subtle (and very often not so subtle) messaging, we are told that being sensitive is a weakness, a flaw, or something to fix or get over. The underlying message being: Who *you are* is flawed; be something else.

It's subtle, but every sensitive soul I have come across has this shared experience of questioning whether their feelings are "right" or "valid," the result being a vast disconnection from and distrust of our own emotional and intuitive guidance. We view it as a flawed system. *No one else seems to feel this way or sense what I am sensing, so I must be wrong.* Many of us also had our spiritual gifts invalidated. Whether it was seeing spiritual beings or being able to see auras, these were chalked up to a wild imagination. Little by little, we end up overriding the very magic we have inside in order to conform to societal expectations. It's a continuous disconnection from our true selves, and it outlines our sensitivity—our gift—as something to be shut down.

Who do you need me to be? I will give up myself to be the person you need until I can't remember who I am.

In order to cope with being deep processors and deep feelers in a world that is uncomfortable with sensitivity, many sensitive souls develop these adaptive strategies for survival. But if you look closer, these patterns just become a ritual of self-abandonment, glorified and reinforced by the cultural messaging that we must value sacrifice, service, or being "good," especially in women.

We learn that being sensitive, or being ourselves, is not accepted, so we turn it off. We disconnect from that piece of us. We build walls around ourselves, we hide our tears, and we suppress our feelings. Over time, our gentle and wide-open hearts become muted under layers of performance. Layer by layer we numb this part of ourselves, and we continue the erosion of ourselves for the benefit of others, losing touch with our inner connection and magic.

Reclaiming the Gift

We may have suppressed it, or ignored it, but the gift is still there. When we learn to honor and care for our unique sensitivity, it becomes a gift, akin to a sixth sense. As empaths, we are naturally "tuned in." We have a deep connection to our inner wisdom, which can be a powerful guiding force in our lives if we remain open to it. We have the ability to read people and the unspoken truths under their words. We are excellent lie detectors. As empowered empaths who are aware of their own energy and behaviors, we can be extremely good at reading the energy in a room or of a person or situation without doubting ourselves.

Here are some of the beautiful gifts within our sensitivity:

- **Deep Empathy:** Our sensitivity allows us to connect with others deeply.
- **Creativity:** As highly sensitive individuals, we possess a deep inner world and are often very creative.

- **Connection to Nature:** We have a deep connection to the earth and animals.
- **Intuitive Ability:** We have a strong connection to our inner wisdom.
- **Ability to Dive Deep:** We are excellent space holders and like to connect on deep levels.
- **Appreciation of Beauty:** We see the magnified beauty of the world in all its details.
- **Psychic or Spiritual Connection:** We have a strong connection to our intuition, and our ability to pick up on subtle information extends beyond our physical environment.

Yes, you are psychic. As I mentioned earlier, the ability to deeply feel others' emotions and physical sensations is one of the gifts I use in my sessions with clients. This ability actually falls under the Clair senses and is known as Clairempathy and Clairsentience (if you ever doubted your sensitivity as a gift!), and I will go into deeper detail on it in Chapter 10. But essentially, Clairempathy and Clairsentience are psychic abilities related to emotional and sensory perception.

Clairempathy: Often described as "clear emotional feeling," it is the extrasensory ability to *perceive* and *understand* the emotional energy of others

- Example: Sensing residual anger in a room after an argument or intuitively feeling a loved one's grief from afar

Clairsentience: The ability to *physically feel* energy, emotions, or sensations from others

- Examples: Absorbing a friend's anxiety and feeling the tightness in your own chest or, on a mediumship level, feeling a deceased person's cause of death—as in my example of not being able to breathe when a client's mother came through

I'll share a personal story here, because with empaths and even highly sensitive people, it's important to understand that not everything we feel is ours to hold. One cold February morning, I opened my eyes and was immediately flooded with despair, a deep heaviness in my whole body; it felt like I couldn't move. I instantly began crying. It was a feeling of complete hopelessness and emptiness that I could not explain. Nothing had happened; I had gone to bed happy; things were going quite well in my personal and professional life. But I couldn't shake it. Tears streamed down my cheeks while I fed the kids breakfast. I knew this feeling wasn't mine. I wasn't sure why, but I had a feeling I should call my mom.

When she answered, she shared the news that a family member I was very close with was in the hospital fighting for her life. The despair and hopelessness that I had been feeling wasn't mine at all; it was an empathic knowing that someone I loved was suffering immensely. This is sometimes referred to as crisis telepathy, or a sudden and intense feeling or knowing that someone you love is in distress. This is the same ability I used when I knew my dad was in distress on the way to the hospital in Chapter 3. We also hear about this very often with twins, when one can feel what the other is feeling even when separated. Or in mothers with their children, whether they are at school or apart, and the mother knows the child is ill or in need of help. This is one reason I believe that being an empath is not always born from trauma and hypervigilance; it's not always about scanning a room or people's faces; sometimes it transcends distance and physical boundaries—because energy transcends physical distance. That's why you can pick up on the energy of the person whose TikTok video you just watched, or why you can experience energy healing work remotely.

For Clairempaths, because we are so tuned in, it is not an uncommon experience, especially with close friends and family, to have a sense or feeling in your body that something has happened even when that person is not in our physical proximity.

Is This Mine?

This is a question I tell clients to ask whenever they feel flooded by emotions or sensations that don't make sense to them: *Is this mine?*

The next time you feel sudden or intense emotions or sensations, place a hand on your heart and take a deep breath in with a long exhale. Then ask yourself, "Is this mine?" and see what comes through for you. Over time, this practice can be an aid in discerning what needs our attention and what can be released. I will acknowledge, though, that it can be difficult to know what is yours and what isn't, especially if you haven't spent much time getting to know your baseline energy, or if you've been stuck in survival mode.

Baseline Energy

I like to think that we all have a baseline energy. Our baseline energy is our true essence, our core state of being. It's the state of our inner energy, unique to each of us. The state when our nervous system is not in survival mode, when we feel safe and free to be our authentic selves. Imagine it as a serene lake with still waters—free from the ripples.

Triggers from life's challenges and interactions can move us, casting ripples on that water, throwing off our baseline energy. That gossipy co-worker, our spouse asking where the scissors are again, an unexpected bill, a traffic jam—all of these things can churn the water—our baseline energy. Global crises, health issues, family dynamics, and even our unmet expectations can also create waves. Now, it's not about always maintaining a state of calm water (which is not possible!); it's about recognizing what is casting those ripples so you can move with it rather than getting stuck in it. When we don't acknowledge these things as they come up, that energy tends to build up in our bodies, causing a sense of imbalance.

Think of your baseline energy as a dynamic equilibrium—a state you continually move in and out of, rather than a fixed point you reach once and for all. It's the rooted and anchored center we return to after life's inevitable disturbances. We can achieve this balanced dance when we begin to choose differently and to move differently in ways that more greatly honor who we are.

We will get more into this when we discuss shadow work in Chapter 9, but for now, let's begin to recognize some of where energy is being exerted.

An Energy Audit Practice

On a sheet of paper or in your notebook, separate the page into three columns. In the first column, make a list of activities you do on a weekly basis. Think about your day-to-day activities; these could be tasks like emptying the dishwasher, commuting to work, interactions with co-workers, being the troop leader for your daughter's Girl Scouts, working out. . . . Whatever it is you do each week, just write it down.

In the middle column, list out activities that feel energizing and rewarding to you.

Some examples might be:

- A quiet cup of coffee
- Painting or drawing
- Cooking while listening to music
- Gathering with friends or loved ones
- Reading a good book

In the final column, list out activities that drain your energy. Some examples might be:

- Overcommitting to things
- Social media scrolling that leaves you feeling less than
- Relationships that feel one-sided
- A cluttered house
- Having no time alone to decompress or reconnect
- Endless negative news cycles

1 = Enjoyable/Energizing
2= Slightly draining
3= Draining
4= Extremely draining

Now, using the key above, rate each of your activities in that first column according to whether they drain you or energize you. Do you have mostly energy-draining activities written down, or is there a good balance?

Look at the tasks or interactions you have listed that are extremely draining and ask yourself these questions:

- Am I abandoning myself and prioritizing others to do this?
- Can I delegate any of these to someone else?
- Is there a way that I can choose differently or prioritize myself while still doing these activities?
- Can I swap some of the energy-draining activities out for some more energizing activities?
- Can I add in more energizing activities?

Be honest with yourself. Some things will be unavoidable, like interactions with co-workers, but we can always choose to move differently. Just noticing and being aware of how we react or respond, how our body feels, or what comes up for us is the first step in shifting out of autopilot. Instead of reacting or playing out old patterns, we can pause and choose to move from a more grounded and conscious place.

Becoming aware of our baseline energy allows us to tune in throughout the day and become more comfortable with understanding our own energy. In moments of overwhelm, do a quick check-in with yourself to determine if what you are feeling is yours or if it belongs to someone else. If the emotion or sensation is not yours, release it by gently placing your hands on your body where you feel the feeling and state out loud, "I release all that is not mine to hold," and feel the weight of it leave your body.

But what if what you're feeling is yours? The key here will be to allow it, not resist it. Resisting our feelings causes us to hold on to them. And the more we resist, the more they brew and the bigger they can become. The phrase "you've got to feel it to heal it" is rooted in truth. This will take practice, especially if you've never allowed space for your own feelings. But I promise it is possible with practice. Talk to the feeling like an old friend and welcome it in. You can say out loud or to yourself, "There is space for you here," and as you do this, sit with the feeling, allowing it to move through you.

Why This Matters

Our thoughts, emotions, and stress levels don't just affect how we *feel*—they can directly impact our immune system. This mind-body connection is well-supported by scientific research. When the nervous system becomes overwhelmed, whether from chronic stress or fear, it can start to weaken our immune defenses.

Science clearly supports this connection: Chronic stress triggers the release of hormones like cortisol, which, over time, can suppress immune function, increase inflammation, and reduce the body's ability to fight off illness.

That's why I believe that energy hygiene, when paired with healthy boundaries and nervous system regulation, is essential for us sensitive souls. So, what are some signs that our energy and nervous system might be calling for some extra care?

- Feeling exhausted
- Having general low energy
- Feeling overwhelmed or on edge
- Feeling irritable
- Having trouble sleeping
- Getting headaches
- Feeling numb

Taking Care of Your Gift

What makes our deep empathy a gift rather than a burden to carry is how we choose to honor and care for it. Think of any other natural-born ability: a pianist who seems to just understand music, or a basketball player whose height and dexterity allow them to breeze down the court. These are gifts they were born with, but they are gifts that become gifts only with intention, practice, and care. Being an empath is no different. Musicians need rehearsal; basketball players need practice; empaths need mindful energy management. Much like athletes strengthen their physical gifts through training regimens, empaths must develop grounding rituals that honor their sensitivity in order to maintain energetic sovereignty.

Empowering Practices

In order to begin healing the sensitivity wound in yourself, you must reclaim your own energy and begin honoring yourself, your energetic needs, and your deeply feeling nature.

There are so many energy protection techniques aimed toward empaths, and while I find some effective (and personally use them), I've come to realize that they only address half the equation. True energetic empowerment is not just about clearing what doesn't belong in our energy field. It requires that we tend to our own internal energetic landscape as well, i.e., our needs, wants, and boundaries. It's about tuning in and listening when our body is communicating, whether it's a clenched jaw or even just shallow breathing. It's about creating safety and presence within ourselves and honoring our sensitive requirements. And it's about showing up for ourselves and rebuilding our self-acceptance and compassion.

I know, for those of us who've navigated life with blurred or nonexistent boundaries, distinguishing between our own energy, or what we want and need, and others' energies can feel nearly impossible. That's why reconnecting with yourself and better understanding your own baseline energy is the first step. This self-awareness becomes your compass, helping you discern what isn't yours to carry, release unnecessary burdens, and move through life from a grounded, supported state.

Let's take a look at some supportive energy hygiene practices along with some nervous system regulation tools, in order to begin fostering the conditions that will allow us to gently reconnect with our gift. And if your energy audit practice was filled with only the draining bits, consider adding some of these practices into your daily or weekly schedule.

Visualization Practices

Visualization is a technique where you create mental images in your mind's eye while engaging other physical sensations, such as feeling or sensing, to fully immerse yourself in the experience. Visualization serves many purposes, but for these practices listed here, we are looking to create calm and balance within the physical and emotional body.

To get started, find a comfortable position, listening deeply to what your body needs in this moment. Enter the space, leaving aside your to-do list and any expectations or judgments. Just practice being present with yourself and your body.

If it feels good for you, you can begin to slow your breath. Breathe in to the count of four, hold for four, and slowly exhale to the count of four. Do a few rounds of this until you feel your energy center.

Grounding: I invite you to imagine your own energy field (think of those energy tendrils) connecting with Earth's energy field. Feel the nurturing and warm energy of Mother Earth surrounding and supporting you. Visualize giant, sturdy roots growing from your tailbone, pushing down into the earth and wrapping around its core. These roots are anchoring you into your space, holding you. Let yourself feel safe, held, and supported.

Cord Cutting: Next, visualize removing any energetic cords that might be keeping you weighed down or feeling stuck. These cords can be emotional, spiritual, energetic, or even just repeated critical thoughts. Think about the energy tendrils we discussed earlier, and perhaps there are a few of them entangled in stuff you want to let go of. Call forward your team of angels, guides, and the higher wisdom within your soul. Feel their deeply loving and supportive energy around you as you say to them, "Thank you, angels and guides, for your support today and for clearing any energetic attachments to stress, anxiety, expectations, judgments, or anything that is weighing on my heart." Feel and visualize those cords severing and falling away from your energy field.

Shielding Technique: After you have cut cords and grounded yourself, visualize the most beautiful healing light pouring from the cosmos above, down through the crown of your head. This light can be any color that comes to mind. Feel this beautiful healing light as it moves from your head, down through your eyes, ears, and throat, clearing any stagnant energy and releasing any tension or weight you may be carrying. Feel it move through your heart center as it clears any fears you are holding. From your heart center now, emit this beautiful healing energy all around you. This is your heart energy—it is pure love. This light emission will not only be your shield from any surrounding energies that you might otherwise pick up, but it will shape your space with love and intention as well.

Do this visualization practice every morning before you leave the house or on your way to work. And again, when you get into bed at night.

I love these practices, but remember, healing and energy empowerment are both an energetic *and* embodied process. It's not simply about clearing what doesn't belong in your energy field and holding your visions; it's also about creating safety and presence within your body. You can clear your energy all day, but without grounding into your body, you're not creating true balance. Energy hygiene and nervous system regulation are partners on the path to true embodiment and empowerment. For a guided version of this visualization practice, download my free Anchored meditation on my website (scan the code below to listen).

Practices for Grounded Connection

Now that we have cleared and released what doesn't belong in our energy fields, it's time to focus on connection and grounded presence, which help to anchor your body and yourself, creating safety, stability, and connection. This next section will guide you through practices that support grounded presence, nervous system regulation, and a deeper relationship with your physical form.

Nervous System Regulation

Nervous system regulation has become a bit of a buzzword, but what does it even mean? Essentially, it's about our ability to maintain balance between our sympathetic (activating) and parasympathetic (calming) systems. It's not about being calm all the time; it's about being flexible to move from a state of stress back into equilibrium. We'll get more into the nervous system and survival states in the next chapter, but for the sake of energy management, it's really about two simple things: slowing down and bringing more mindfulness and presence into our lives. That's it. Simple, but not necessarily easy, especially if you're constantly in a state of activation.

What we want to create, using the following practices, is space for safety and deeper connection.

Supportive Self-Touch

As empaths, we've spent a lifetime tuning in to others. Supportive self-touch is a gentle way for us to reconnect with our physical bodies and energy. It can also signal safety to our nervous systems, which promotes a sense of calm. This doesn't have to be an Olympic event; even a small gesture or movement can have a deep impact. Here are a few practices to try:

- **Self-hug:** Wrapping your arms around yourself, gently squeeze your upper arms and shoulders. Connect with your breath and notice how it feels to simply hold yourself.
- **Arm stroking:** Using the palm of your hand, try to gently and slowly stroke from one shoulder down to your wrist, then switch sides. This gentle touch helps regulate your nervous system by engaging the parasympathetic (rest and digest) response.
- **Hand on heart or belly:** Gently place a hand over your heart or on your belly and connect with your breathing. Notice the warmth of your hand and the gentle rise and fall of your belly. Can you also tune in to your own energy?

As you engage in reconnection with yourself and your own body, the most important thing will be following your own cues. Listen to your needs and what feels right. The goal is to create safety and support, reminding your system that you are here, and you are cared for.

Meditation

Meditation can help us reduce stress, improve focus, and be able to tap in to our inner wisdom. It is a practice in witnessing what is: allowing our thoughts and feelings to be and simply noticing them. It is not about clearing the mind or transcending to enlightenment. The most difficult aspect of developing a meditation practice for a lot of people can be the stillness and connection. So, if this is a practice you want to develop in yourself, start small: Set a timer. You can start with one minute or five minutes, whatever you feel is achievable. We'll go deeper into the practice of meditation in Chapter 10.

Create a Ritual

Many of our daily routines are rooted in ritual. Consider your morning routine: Do you always reach for a certain mug to drink your coffee from? What are your favorite birthday traditions? What holiday customs do you hold dear? What makes something a ritual, versus simply a routine or habit, lies in the mindfulness and intention we infuse into our actions.

Having a daily ritual can be a powerful way to show ourselves care and reduce stress. It offers predictability and routine, gives us something to look forward to, and builds a sense of structure.

Rituals offer a plethora of benefits, including:

- **Improved Mental Well-Being**: Rituals have been shown to enhance mood and overall mental well-being.
- **Increased Energy**: A consistent practice can help clear our energy and prepare us for our day.

- **Mindfulness and Stress Reduction**: Rituals encourage us to be present, which has been shown to lower stress levels.
- **Self-Prioritization**: Rituals create a space where we can prioritize ourselves and increase introspection.
- **Spiritual Connection**: This sacred space allows for a greater connection to our spirit team and a higher power.
- **Anxiety Reduction:** Engaging in rituals has been shown to lower anxiety levels, especially during stressful times or times of transition.

For your ritual, decide what time it will start. I like to set my alarm before my kids wake up, light some candles, and play gentle, soothing music while I pour myself a cup of coffee in my favorite mug. It's simple, and I start my day with intention and purpose rather than rushing around to take care of everyone else first.

You can include things like keeping phones or screens off for a set amount of time, lighting candles, journaling, taking a bath, reflecting on what went well in your day, gentle stretching, or a warm cup of tea. Choose elements that are soothing for you and will be achievable to replicate each day or week. I have listed a few energy hygiene ideas that you can incorporate into your ritual if they speak to you.

Energy Cleansing Ritual Ideas

Salt Bath: Salt and water have been used for centuries across cultures for purification. Make sure you allow yourself some alone time in a private space so you won't be disturbed. Light candles, keep lights low or off, and make the atmosphere as relaxing as possible. You can add in some essential oils as well. Set an intention like "I release what no longer serves me," and visualize any energy stagnation dissolving as you soak. For those without access to a bath, you can try a foot soak with warm water and salt while visualizing energy flowing out through your feet.

Smudging: Smudging is a Native American tradition of cleansing energy from a space using the smoke from a sacred plant. White sage and palo santo are probably the most well-known; however, there are more sustainable and ethical options that work just as well. Dried rosemary has worked well for me. When using smoke to cleanse your space, it is important to set an intention to remove any negative or unwanted energies. Moving slowly through your space, you can ask your angels or spirit guides to assist in removing anything from your energetic space that is not serving your highest good.

Alone Time: Solitude is a must for us sensitives. It's not about isolating but about intentional reconnection to ourselves. Time alone and in silence is like an automatic recharge of our energy. Setting aside time each day to be in connection with ourselves is important. It doesn't have to be long; even just five minutes of sacred silence in the morning is energizing. Alone time can happen even in shared spaces. Try noise-canceling headphones or a calming playlist to create a bit of mental solitude.

Movement: Movement can be a great practice for releasing energies. Have you ever needed to go for a run to clear your head? Or felt lighter after an impromptu dance party with your kids? It's because we hold on to energy and emotions in our physical bodies. Movement can be anything you are comfortable with. It could be jumping up and down, shaking, dancing, running, or simple and gentle movements. Anything that gets the physical body moving will help to release stuck energy. And if movement is not available to you, consider visualizing the sensation of motion: Imagine your breath guiding energy flow, or visualize a "shake-out" of tension from your body. The goal is to connect with your body in ways that feel safe and empowering, honoring your unique needs.

Decluttering: Our physical spaces are an extension of our energetic space. That's why when we clear out all the clutter and tidy things, we just feel lighter. When decluttering, start small; don't set out to declutter the whole house. Choose a room, or a section, and mindfully make decisions to let go of what needs letting go of. When decluttering, I think it's important not to simply throw stuff in a box and shove it in the back of a closet. It's still there, taking up physical and mental space. Really think about what is serving a purpose in your life, and what is just stuff taking up valuable real estate in your mind and physical space.

Detox from Screens: We do not need to be physically in someone's presence to pick up their energy. We can do this scrolling social media. As sensitives, we might be unknowingly absorbing the energy of a person or a highly charged post, and that stays with us. Next time you are scrolling, just notice how your breathing changes with all the talking heads going by. The Internet is like a giant pool of energy, swirling about. Taking breaks from social media can be very effective in cleansing our energetic fields. You might also consider curating your social feeds to prioritize uplifting accounts and mute energy-draining, negative, or fear-inducing content.

Time in Nature: Spending time in nature offers a deep sense of grounding and renewal. The gentle stillness of trees and the soothing songs of birds have been scientifically shown to reduce stress and promote calmness. Whether it's the fresh air in wide open spaces or the simple act of feeling sunlight on your skin, nature helps release stagnant energy and refresh your spirit. Even brief moments like sitting by a window with a view of greenery or listening to natural sounds can provide a restorative connection, no matter where you are.

Think of your ritual as a gentle act of self-care, a way to reset, recharge, and reconnect with your inner self and energy. Experiment with what resonates for you, and remember, it's about presence and consistency, not about making them perfect.

Key Takeaways

Until now, being highly sensitive, or an empath, might have felt like a burden that you carry. You might look around and think life would be so much easier if you just felt *less*. I get it. For most of my life, I felt very out of place, like something was wrong with me because I couldn't seem to manage the activities and environments that others navigated with such ease. What I didn't realize then is that I wasn't defective; I was simply a highly sensitive and intuitive empath trying to survive in a world that hadn't taught me how to honor my gifts.

Overriding our sensitivity to "fit in" is an exhausting performance, one that inevitably leads to burnout. But being highly sensitive is not a flaw that needs fixing; it's an extraordinary gift that, if honored and cared for, can be a beautiful compass for deeper connection, creativity, and intuition. It's okay to move at a slower pace, to prioritize your energy, and to listen to your own needs.

True energy empowerment is *both* an energetic and embodied process. It's not simply about clearing what doesn't belong in your energy field, but also about creating safety and presence within your body. Energy hygiene, self-compassion, connection, and nervous system regulation are all partners on the path to true energy empowerment. They help us clear what isn't ours to carry while grounding us in the wisdom of our bodies. This is where we can begin to release the old patterns of people pleasing and perfectionism. This is where we reclaim our power.

But how did we become so disconnected from our sensitivity and ourselves? The answer lies in a world that often teaches us to distrust (or hate) our bodies, silence our intuition, and equate self-sacrifice with worthiness. It's a world that pedals fear and doom and gloom, often hijacking our ability to be present and connected.

In the next chapter, we'll explore this fear and disconnection, tracing the roots from societal conditioning to trauma responses, and uncover how our innate gifts became buried under layers of survival. Most importantly, we'll continue the healing journey of coming home to our bodies and our spirits.

6

Healing the Connection Wound

Reframing Fear and Reconnecting Mind, Body, and Spirit

Hope is my guide.
When fear was my chauffeur,
I lost sight of hope;
it was too hard to see her in the fog.

Now fear is my passenger,
and hope is my guiding light—
not fleeting or shaky,
but an anchor.

It is a knowing,
stretching from my ancestors' roots,
reaching into the future,
beyond what I can see,
where it will continue to shine: a legacy of light.

We connect to the divine and to our own magic by reconnecting to and loving ourselves.

We are wired for survival. This is part of our humanness. But what happens when we get stuck in this survival? When it's no longer helping us but keeping us stuck?

I mentioned earlier in the book that when my spiritual abilities opened up in my early 20s, it was the same month the chronic infections started. When I shut my abilities down five years later, the chronic infections disappeared that same month. And when my mediumship abilities opened back up again, the infections started again.

I couldn't explain it at the time, but I began to realize this wasn't simply a coincidence. What did my abilities and these symptoms have in common?

They were messengers.

They were highlighting a deep fear I was holding on to within my body. Across the next few chapters, fear will be a big theme woven throughout, because it can become a huge disconnector between ourselves, our intuition, and even truth. There is no shortage of fear in our modern world; in fact, fear tactics have been used for centuries as a means to rule or control by hijacking the very instincts meant to protect us. We'll get into the use of fear historically to disconnect us from our own magic in Chapter 8 when we talk about the Witch Wound. But fear is very commonly used today to create confusion and disconnection. The constant activation of fear, whether through media, divisive politics, or even daily micro-stressors from scrolling online, can keep us in a heightened state of alertness, eroding our ability to feel safe, make clear decisions, and even connect with our inner wisdom.

By definition, fear is an intense emotion triggered by the detection of a threat, which activates an alarm reaction geared to prioritize our survival. This is hardwired into us as humans, and we need it to keep us safe. This healthy activation to threat keeps us from burning our hand on a hot stove or walking into oncoming traffic.

But what about when it becomes chronic? Or when there is no real threat at all?

This was my case: Fear had taken over.

Spirit Intervenes

One hot July night I woke and sensed another urinary tract infection coming on. I had just resolved the last one and felt myself begin to panic. If you've experienced any chronic health issues, you know the visceral panic that can occur with a flare-up. It was the middle of the night, I had no way to stop it or relieve the pain, and I could physically feel fear beginning to flood my body. In desperation, I just placed my hands on my stomach and began praying for healing. I visualized this fear collecting as a dark-gray cloud in the center of my abdomen, under where I had placed my hands.

As I did this, the ceiling of my bedroom opened up, and a being in bright yellow light appeared above me. It began surrounding me in a warm, healing energy. The being was incredibly peaceful, and I could feel its energy radiating through my whole body, like it was being infused into me.

I instantly felt my body relax.

This being assured me, "It's okay. I'm here to help," and I intuitively knew it was going to help me release this cloud of fear pooling in my stomach. It then instructed, "Now take a deep breath," and when I obeyed, I could feel this fear-cloud in my abdomen balloon up like a pregnant belly. Then the being said, "Release," and as I exhaled, the cloud completely evaporated. The being was gone, and my room had returned to normal. I lay there awhile, feeling both in awe and at peace until I finally fell back to sleep.

The next morning, I woke up with no sign of infection and with a whole new understanding and clarity about how much fear was affecting my life. Not just fear for my health, but a deep fear that I had been carrying for a very long time.

The Impact of Fear

With recurring symptoms, I had been meeting my body's requests to witness, to heal, and even to feel, with self-punishment and force. I transferred my fears onto ingredient labels. I panicked about any physical sensations. I worried about the words I said out loud and what people would think; I was even afraid of my ability to connect with spirit.

Everything felt like a threat.

I realized after that spirit visitation that not only had I been carrying this fear with me for a lifetime, letting it call all the shots, but I was perpetuating it with the constant stress of trying to heal.

Let's look at what happens in the body when we feel fear, specifically related to the nervous system. Our nervous system is a beautiful and complex system responsible for almost everything in our bodies. The **sympathetic nervous system** is the body's fight-or-flight response. It is responsible for activation of the stress response to prepare us for threat or danger.

The **parasympathetic nervous system** is what our bodies return to after a threat. It is responsible for slowing down our breathing and heart rate, for our digestion, for nutrient absorption, and even for healing and immune function.

In a state of sympathetic nervous system activation, our bodies produce increased cortisol and adrenaline (epinephrine), which can contribute to inflammation in the body. But when we get stuck here, in this continuous activated state, or when we are chronically stressed or afraid, we are no longer in balance between the two. We'll get into the different survival responses in the next chapter, but let's take a look at the sympathetic versus parasympathetic nervous system activation symptoms here.

Symptoms of sympathetic nervous system activation	Symptoms of parasympathetic nervous system activation
Increased heart rate	Decreased heart rate
Elevated blood pressure	Lowered blood pressure
Rapid or shallow breathing	Slowed breathing
Muscle tension	Relaxed muscles
Heightened alertness	Promotion of rest and recovery
Decreased digestion	Increased digestion/nutrient absorption
Release of stress hormones	Improved immune function

If you look at the body response related to each, it makes perfect sense why slowing down, becoming present, and even being gentle with ourselves can be so crucial on our healing journeys. It's something that took me literal decades (and help from a spiritual being) to actually understand and implement for myself. I'm hoping I can save you the time with this chapter.

All those healing regimens, books I read, intense protocols, detoxes, cleanses, oil pulling—I was just reiterating to myself that I was broken and needing fixing, and that fixing was going to come from force. Always trying to strongarm myself into healing, I tried everything.

Everything but slowing down.

Which brings me to fear and chronic stress as disconnectors. As I mentioned earlier, fear activates our fight-or-flight response, but what does that have to do with our ability to access our inner wisdom or feel connected to ourselves? Think about what happens physiologically, in your body, when you feel threatened or afraid:

- A tightness in your chest (chest)
- A knot in your stomach (stomach)
- Racing thoughts (mind)
- Shallow breathing (breath)

Stress hormones are actually interfering or suppressing the signals from the areas of our body that receive intuitive insights: our heart center and our gut.

Think about where intuition or inner wisdom shows up in the body:

- An expansion in your heart center (chest)
- A knowing in your gut (stomach)
- A soft, guiding voice (mind)
- A calm feeling (slow breathing)

Our inner wisdom is often described as a still, small voice. There is a reason we hear it when we are in stillness, meditation, or quiet reflection. Those are the moments when it isn't being drowned out by the static of fear or the hustle and bustle of life. Fear leaves us feeling ungrounded or spiraling in worry, which is the exact opposite of the conditions that foster our ability to listen within. I'll go deeper into how to tell the difference between the fear voice and the intuitive voice in Chapter 10, as it's a question I get asked often.

Rest, stillness, and moving gently are pivotal for shifting us out of the survival response and into a more mindful space where we can begin to feel into our bodies and dip into this inner landscape. But it can be so hard to move toward rest when we are hypervigilant or are so used to chronic stress, constant busyness, and fear.

The Challenge of Rest

I remember in Glennon Doyle's book *Untamed*, the author described how her wife, Abby, could just fall asleep on the couch in the middle of the day, and how this act of rest would fill Glennon with rage. I laughed out loud because I could totally resonate with this, as I also have a spouse capable of sleeping anytime, anywhere, and it often fills me with rage. I mean, the man falls asleep on the couch while the kids are climbing on him, on a moving train surrounded by strangers . . . literally anywhere, anytime is a good place for him to feel relaxed enough to sleep.

Glennon went on to explain that the rage she felt wasn't actually because Abby had perfected rest; it was because rest was something Glennon couldn't allow for herself, and my gosh, I felt that in my core.

How do people *relax*? And where do they even get the audacity to relax?

Even after a hot bubble bath, in my softest pj's, surrounded by candlelight and calming music, my body would reject this idea of rest. I would sit down and then get right back up to move the laundry or decide to organize my sock drawer, anything to keep moving and keep busy. My mind couldn't relax either; sitting down was like its cue to bring up that one time someone complimented my bangs and I replied with "Thanks, I have a big forehead," or just in general all the things I should be worrying about, just in case!

Rest felt hard. But on a deeper level, rest felt dangerous.

There was a time that I might have described this inability to rest as me being ambitious, or a real go-getter! Or any other glamorizing word for what was really happening, which was that I was stuck in this activation state.

If you were a highly sensitive child who grew up around chaos, dysfunction, or even just in an unsafe environment, it makes sense that you learned to brace for the next outburst, the next screaming match, the next critical remark thrown your way, or sometimes worse. Resting wasn't safe because you had to be prepared, always hypervigilant and "on." Or maybe you were even shamed for resting; if a parent or caregiver saw you sitting down and called you lazy or immediately gave you something to get up and do, you internalized that as rest is bad and productivity is good. And your body is storing that memory.

Add to this the cultural narrative that rest equals laziness and that constant productivity is the ultimate measure of worth and success, or that we must earn our rest through productivity, and it's no wonder so many of us struggle to truly relax.

Add it to the list of methods we learned to armor ourselves with. These protective mechanisms were meant to shield and protect us from harm, which may have been vital in childhood or unsafe environments. Yet these same survival strategies now keep us trapped in a cycle of hypervigilance and relentless preparation for the unknown.

But our disconnection is impacted by more than these internal patterns. Even if we had caregivers that modeled rest, beyond our own experiences lies a modern system designed to hijack our nervous system: a 24/7 culture of fear-based media cycles, political polarization, urgent notifications, and micro-stressors that keep us scrolling, striving, and bracing for the next threat. We are often face-to-face with chronic manufactured stress, fear, and urgency that disconnects us from ourselves and even others.

Modern Disconnection

"I'm going to miss the stress" were the words I uttered to a friend when I was walking away from corporate life in New York City to move to Hong Kong. And they were true words. I already had a sense of unease about not being connected to the constant ping of "urgent" e-mails, the incessant honking of taxi cabs, or the stress of employee issues to take on every day. Perhaps, on some level, I knew that stillness would call me inward to witness things I had been using stress to avoid.

We're taught to avoid our inner world from a young age. In the classrooms we're taught to sit still when our bodies want to move. We're taught to be quiet when our voices want to be heard. We're taught to neglect our bodily functions, like the need to urinate, in order to not be disruptive in class. We are kept busy with sports and extracurricular activities, shoving dinner into our mouths while we cram in homework. Then we enter the workforce, and we work ourselves overtime; we wake before our bodies are ready; we stay up too late after a full day of work and chauffeuring kids and making dinner because we want just a moment to ourselves so we have to steal it from our own sleep cycle, and even that we will use to stare at nightmarish news headlines.

We are chronically stressed and emotionally numb from processing a constant onslaught of information. Everything feels urgent, and we never have time to process what we're taking in, so we just feel overloaded and overwhelmed. We are going through the motions, but we lack true purpose, true soul alignment. And if we think about that for too long, it all feels hopeless, so we open our phones and scan, waiting for someone to tell us what to do, give us the answers, tell us how to feel better. We'll look anywhere but inward, because often, that is the hardest place to look.

Pause.

Notice your own body and breathing after reading through that section. What do you feel? Perhaps constricted and tense? Maybe you stopped breathing altogether. Place a hand on your heart and just reconnect with your body and breath.

Feel the difference?

I did miss the stress, at first. But as I learned to rest, moving ever more gently and slowly, I began to see how the stress had been controlling me. It became more and more obvious how pervasive fear and stress culture were, and I didn't want that anymore. I wanted to move differently. But to do that, I had to start choosing differently.

If you're reading this book, you've probably heard the calling, the pull inward, or an overall invitation to come home to yourself. And it makes sense, because so many of us have been living in this chronic disconnection but are waking up to the fact that it's not what we want for ourselves.

Chronic symptoms, chronic stress, chronic anxiety can all be a sign that we are disconnected, that there is a disconnection between our mind, body, and soul. Our overwhelm often comes from this disconnection, this split between our own inner knowing, our wants and needs, and how we are showing up.

This modern disconnection is not a mistake. The systems in place thrive when we are in disconnection and depletion. When we're untethered from our inner wisdom, because when fear and overwhelm dominate, we become more susceptible to external narratives about who we should be, what we should want, and what we should buy.

But the moment we pause, become aware of this, and begin to reconnect with our deepest truths, remembering our inherent wholeness, we reclaim agency over our lives, clarity in our choices, and even our spiritual and psychic abilities. This is why so many people awakened to their abilities during the COVID lockdowns in 2020. It was a time of forced stillness; many highly sensitive people turned to meditation and mindfulness practices to help reduce stress, and subsequently reconnected to their own innate psychic abilities.

Connection

The law of vibration suggests that all energy moves at specific frequencies, with fear being among the lowest. This heavy vibration can feel like a cloud, making it impossible to tune in to our inner wisdom. When we're trapped in fear's frequency, we can become stuck in overwhelm, uncertainty, and worry.

Hope, on the other hand, carries a higher vibrational frequency. This lighter frequency makes it easier to tune in to the sacred space of self-connection. Hope is one of the most important things to hold in your heart when navigating your own healing or awakening. This is not about forcing "high vibes only" positivity, as we've explored the importance of not spiritually bypassing our own emotions or experiences. We're not shoving down lower frequency emotions; we can make space for them without letting them run the show. This is about recognizing we are multifaceted, honoring the protective nature of fear and our beautifully designed nervous system, while also understanding how these responses can influence our own regulation and connection, both to ourselves and the world around us.

The law of vibration looks at frequency, but let's consider how sound, intentions, and environmental energy can all directly impact and even alter physical structures of things like water and the human body. If we look at sound wave healing, or vibrational medicine, we know that different frequencies will interact with cellular vibrations in the body. That's why tools, like sound bowls or tuning forks, are used in healing.

But what about just the words we speak or even simply our intentions? In the 1990s, Dr. Masaru Emoto, a Japanese researcher who studied the effects of human consciousness on water molecules, conducted a study where he would expose different samples of water to specific words, phrases, and even thoughts and intentions. He then froze the water and studied the crystalline structure that formed in freezing. The water that was exposed to words of love and gratitude formed beautiful and symmetrical crystals, while the water that was exposed to hate and loathing formed irregular and almost grotesque crystalline structures. The study concluded that words and intentions can indeed impact the molecular structure of water molecules.

Now consider that we, as humans, are made up of almost 70 percent water. Our own critical thoughts, internal judgments, and self-loathing can very well be impacting our bodies and our own frequency. As highly sensitive folks, we already know this is true. Think about how listening to certain music can impact how we feel. Certain tones and notes can bring tears to our eyes, whereas other songs can leave us feeling empowered or calm.

Now, at this point in the book, I hope it's clear that I am not saying, "Hey, just stop being afraid and everything will work out." Unfortunately, for anyone who has been in the grip of anxiety or stuck in survival states, you know it's not that easy. What we want to be doing is fostering our awareness of and connection to ourselves, to how we feel, to the messages of our own energy and bodies, and staying open and curious, allowing things to move through us. It's so important, when doing any of this work, to move gently. Which brings us to gentle connection.

Let's look at what I mean when I say connection. Self-connection can best be thought of as the practice of tuning in to our physical sensations, emotions, truth, inner wisdom, and higher selves, or souls. It happens through thoughtful presence, in safety, and in stillness. It is in developing practices that support this, that we can begin to unearth our truth and move in greater alignment with ourselves.

Coming Back into Connection

Reconnecting with yourself can feel a bit difficult at first, so again, move gently and follow your own lead. I'll share a personal example. After living most of my life very disconnected from my body, and leaving the stress of corporate NYC, I found myself in more and more body-based and mindful spaces. Being present and connecting with myself was quite tricky for me at first.

In the middle of my yoga teacher training, surrounded by 40 other students, lying on my mat, I went through my first-ever guided meditation. Not the best place to start for someone who rejected stillness and connection. Listening as the instructor guided us inward, I was trying to be a "good student," but my body was sounding the alarm, saying, *this isn't safe.*

I didn't want to disrupt anyone else's meditation by moving, and I definitely didn't want to get in trouble, so I sat there while my heart rate increased and my breathing grew shallow, and the anxiety was moving like waves through my body. I felt hot; my skin was flushing; my body was saying, "Get out!"

The exit was right there; I could have listened to my internal alarm system and removed myself, but I stayed, because I didn't want to "fail" or let anyone down, and because I still didn't know how to follow myself or the cues of my body.

Maybe you can relate?

Meditation is difficult; it asks us to connect with ourselves, to sit with ourselves, and to notice our thoughts. When we have spent our whole lives disconnecting from all of that, it can feel like too much. Which is why moving slowly is so important. When we can become gentle with ourselves and make space to check in with our mind, body, and soul, we can begin to see how they are all connected. And how pushing ourselves beyond our capacity or talking to ourselves in a critical or negative way is going to affect everything from our physical to our mental health.

Being in connection means learning to speak the language of our bodies and inner wisdom. It means honoring ourselves when those alarm bells go off instead of overriding them. It's a daily choice to move with ourselves instead of against ourselves. We'll go deeper into listening to the body's signals in the next chapter, but let's look at some practices that can help us begin to move more gently and reclaim our connection.

Some examples include:

- Meditation
- Journaling
- Mindful movement
- Breath work
- Time in nature

I provide a free Gentle Living Guide on my website (QR code on page 116), which contains simple daily prompts for developing a stronger, more compassionate connection to yourself. Whatever practice speaks to you, start small. Think of it as building a relationship with yourself and your body.

You wouldn't meet someone on the street and decide to move in together; you might first ask them for coffee. Reconnection with yourself can be the same because it's often meeting yourself for the first time, so get to know yourself in mini mindful moments.

Gentle Living and Mindfulness Practices

If connection is rooted in presence and safety, how can we begin to intentionally create more moments like this in our daily lives? Where do we start? Let's look at three big ones: rest, joy, and honoring ourselves.

Intentional Rest

In a world that glorifies hustle culture and relies on our disconnection from ourselves, choosing gentleness and ease becomes a sort of rebellion. We've been force-fed the lie that our productivity is what determines our worth and our right to rest. Or we've used busyness to numb the calling from within. Whatever the reason, when we don't know how to rest, we will have to be very intentional with carving out time to relax and practicing the relaxing part, without getting up to move the laundry.

Start by carving intentional pauses, whether through evening rituals like candlelit journaling or phone-free spaces, to begin to create a sense of safety and stillness. Start small; set a timer for five minutes.

Just as rest can feel uncomfortable after years of stress and activation, allowing ourselves to feel joy can be surprisingly challenging.

Choosing Joy

I would argue that, if you've been living in chronic stress or activation, joy can be as challenging as rest. For a long time, it was a running joke between my husband and me that I didn't really know how to feel (or express) joy or excitement. The biggest, most exciting thing could happen to us, and the most I would be able to muster would be a performative "Yes! That's great!"

When I would achieve big goals, I would barely process what I had accomplished before moving on to the next goal, because it not only never felt like enough; I was always waiting for the other shoe to drop.

Joy felt like a part of myself I just couldn't access. Was it even possible? It became a joke between us, but I quite literally didn't know how to let myself feel joy and excitement. It felt like a part of me couldn't trust it, like joy could be taken away, and in order to protect myself from that devastation, I wouldn't let myself feel it to begin with. Healing our relationship with play and joy is just as important as any other part of this journey.

Not only because when we experience joy, our brain releases chemicals like serotonin and dopamine, and joy is known to lower stress levels, boost our immune systems, and even lower pain levels, but because joy is a part of life. When was the last time you gave yourself full permission to prioritize your own joy? Think about it. It's probably been a while. What is one thing you can do today just for the pure joy of it?

Some ideas to inspire you:

- Buy yourself a coffee.
- Watch cute videos of cats (science has shown that watching cute animals decreases our heart rate and blood pressure and even anxiety).
- Do something that makes you laugh.
- Try something new you've been wanting to experience.
- Find your flow state in a hobby or creative activity.
- Move your body joyfully.

Can you try to choose one small act of joy every day?

As we begin to invite more rest and joy into our lives, we'll undoubtedly come up against old stories and beliefs about it. it's important to remember that our struggles with these are often shaped from our early experiences. To truly embrace rest and joy, we may need to reach back and have a conversation with the younger version of ourselves who first learned to shut these down.

Write a Letter to Your Younger Self

The younger version of you might be the version who learned survival over play or rest. She kept you safe. Maybe she is still clutching a blanket over her head as voices rise downstairs. Or she is putting on her best smile to hide her tears on the school bus. Or she is packing her own lunch because her caregivers were absent. Whatever the story, she was doing her best. But she doesn't need to hold the fear anymore. You are here now.

Can you acknowledge her? Perhaps with "I see how hard you worked to keep us safe" or "What happened was not your fault" or "Your anger is safe here." Take some time to feel into what she needs. Reflect on what you may have needed to hear as a child, some comforting words, or an acknowledgement of her strength. If it feels right, grab a piece of paper and write her a letter, acknowledging her. Write freely, just letting the words come through.

As you begin to choose differently for yourself, this might bring an increased effort for your inner child to want to stay safe. As I embarked on bigger and bigger versions of success for myself, I would often wake up in the middle of the night braced for danger. I feared what sort of angry client messages waited in my inbox, or how many trolls had plastered my social media with angry comments. They were imagined storms, but they felt like real threats to me. It took a lot of inner work to realize I was holding a deep-rooted fear that my very existence was dangerous. Little me was bracing for the confirmation that my work, and myself, were a threat to others. It didn't help to ignore her, or to simply tell her there was nothing to worry about. I had to invite her in and give her space, while not allowing her fears to be in charge. One way I did this was by including a photo of my younger self on my desk with the words "*There is room for you here, but we are safe*" written on it. We'll go deeper into this type of work in Chapter 9, but perhaps there is a little you needing to feel safe as well. Can you make space for them?

These practices aren't about adding more to your already full plate; they are about finding space to press Pause and finding the magic in the ordinary moments we've been taught to rush through. When resistance arises (and it will), hear it as your protective parts and your younger self. Thank them by stating, *"I know you're scared. But I can hold us now."*

Key Takeaways

Fear and survival mode, the very thing designed to protect us, can interrupt or fragment our connection to ourselves when we get stuck there. We can become stuck in our protective patterns, in our hypervigilance, or simply on autopilot, trying to keep ourselves safe while simultaneously creating a sense of unsafety within. Some of the fear we carry might be a remembered fear, where our bodies and minds are replaying old ways that kept us safe. But a lot of the fear we face today is manufactured for the sole purpose of keeping us focused outward, worried, and confused. I want you to consider why that might be. Perhaps because if you were deeply connected to your own inner wisdom, strength, and potential and could access this from a rooted and regulated place, you would be incredibly powerful.

So, I pose this question to you: What if the path home to ourselves and our true inner power is not in doing more, or finding the key, but in doing less? Perhaps true health and wellness is not found in another protocol, a new modality, or the latest trends, but a return to self, a turning inward and remembering that we already have the tools within.

When I stopped forcing my healing through rigid rules and began replacing the feeling of "never enough" and "not safe" with increased self-compassion and ease, my body began to find a balance again. Gentle living isn't a lazy or passive experience; it's a choice we make for ourselves. It's choosing to pause; it's choosing what we allow into our homes, our energetic space, our mental space. It's choosing moments of connection over modern micro-stressors and questioning the urgency and fear that is fed to us. And this isn't to say that our journey will magically be easy, or that we should ignore hard things, but it's about meeting ourselves in those challenging moments with grace. Look for yourself at some of the activities or practices in your life. Become mindful of the urgency with which you move through your day and question if it's necessary. How do you relate to fear and how can you choose more peace within your own life?

As we move into deeper connection with ourselves, we inevitably come back into our bodies, which might feel like a foreign place at first. Our bodies can hold on to our stories, communicating in a language we often never learned to speak. In the next chapter, we'll dive deeper into the wisdom of our bodies, exploring how tension patterns, survival responses, and the echoes of adverse childhood experiences can shape our well-being. But by learning to connect with and speak the language of our bodies, we can begin to feel and release what no longer serves us and reconnect with a deeper wisdom within.

7

Healing the Body Wound

Listening to Your Body's Wisdom

My body has held so much.

It has held my truths and my memories; it has absorbed my anger and weathered my emotions. It has endured my hunger and anxiety. It has carried my babies and nurtured new life. It has grown, stretched, grieved, and transformed.

My body has held so much. Coming home to myself has meant coming home to my body—finding safety within it, sitting with discomfort in it, letting myself feel joy in it, and supporting it as it continues to change and carry me.

My body has held so much,

and part of my healing has been mending the relationship with my body.

Listening to its signals, partnering with it, and loving it.

Life is a journey that can be full of beauty and joy, as well as complications and adversity. Within this next chapter, I will be discussing the deeper role of societal conditioning, trauma, and adversity on our relationship with our body. Why am I talking so much about fear and stress in this part of the book? Because it's impossible to talk about the loss of connection to ourselves, and our bodies, without having an understanding of the impact of our experiences, how we hold them, and how they shape us. As humans, we have all experienced adversity in one form or another. Move through this chapter gently, and if it brings up too much for you, skip to the next section. Follow your own lead, as that is the sole purpose of this book.

Holding

"What are you holding on to so tightly?" she asked me.

Lying naked except for the familiar medical gown strategically covering my top and bottom, I watched the little green mechanical stars dancing across the ceiling. I was receiving an abdominal and womb healing massage from an experienced body therapist to help alleviate some of my menstrual symptoms. But this was not the first healing practitioner to ask me this exact question.

What am I holding on to? I thought about it.

Everything?

I had never been what you would call a healthy kid. Not that I had any serious medical diagnoses; I was just always kind of sick. I seemed susceptible to everything. To put it another way, if I'd lived through the Oregon Trail days, I would probably have been the first to die of dysentery, a fact my friends loved to jokingly remind me of.

I had persistent strep throat from childhood into college. My body had become so battered by strep infections that my doctor said it was causing swelling around my heart. I had a diagnosis of juvenile rheumatoid arthritis. I struggled with debilitating menstrual cycles, as well as urinary tract infections that dated back to as early as age seven.

But, as you recall, the month I moved into my studio apartment was the month the physical symptoms began to run my life. We know this was also the same month spirit began visiting. The next decade would have me in and out of doctors' offices, seeing specialists, having lab work done, and being told over and over and over again that everything seemed normal and they didn't know what was wrong.

There were nights I just cried into my pillow out of sheer discomfort and helplessness. I spent hundreds of hours typing my symptoms into search engines, falling into symptom rabbit holes, researching, trying to find anyone else on this planet who might be going through what I was going through. I was in so much physical discomfort and feeling so completely at the mercy of my symptoms. It was exhausting, draining, and overwhelming. I couldn't see an end in sight. The more my symptoms would flare, the more hypervigilant I would become to what I was eating, what I was wearing, and what I was feeling physically—any little sign of tension in my body would send me into a panic that another wave of infections was coming. I felt alone, because there was no one who seemed to be able to help me, and I would throw myself into protocols or regimens that promised relief, only to be let down.

But as I continued to practice slowing down and tuning in with curiosity, I began to notice something: a tension in my lower abdomen. This sensation would flare up in specific situations: when I felt unheard, when I hesitated to speak up, or when someone intentionally crossed my boundaries. It was a physical bracing, a tightening that seemed to lodge itself in my body and linger. I noticed that, within days of this tension building, I'd inevitably develop a urinary tract infection. Over time, I realized this wasn't random; it happened repeatedly, like a pattern I could no longer ignore.

As I discussed in the previous chapter, with the help of spirit intervention, I began to realize the root of this tension was fear, and the pattern was self-abandonment.

Psychosomatics

The term *psychosomatic* refers to the mind-body connection of physical symptoms, where symptoms arise in the body that have a psychological trigger or root cause, like stress or emotional issues. The symptoms are real; they manifest as true issues in the body, but treatment often needs to involve a holistic approach incorporating both body and mind.

I want to be very clear that I do not think negative emotions cause our illnesses or that we cause our own illnesses. I don't even like the term *negative emotions*; all emotions are valid and deserve space, and some illness or disease is simply that, and we don't know what the cause is. I do believe in some situations, that suppressing ourselves, or the holding in and pushing down of *any* emotion, even those deemed "positive" like joy, can impact our bodies. This suppression and holding in is like trying to push a lid onto a boiling pot: It wants to come out.

The most important thing I want you to take away from this chapter is compassion for yourself and how you have so bravely navigated all of life's circumstances. It is only from a place of compassion that we can begin to view some of the pieces of us that want to be known. Now, let's look at beauty standards and suppression.

Beauty Standards and Suppression

From early childhood, we as women are often conditioned to look and behave a certain way. From impossible beauty standards that tell us what size and shape we should be, to the volume of our voice, we are taught to suppress ourselves. This suppression can show up in many ways, from keeping our thoughts and opinions to ourselves to extreme dieting; it's as if we begin to erase who we are. For women from marginalized or minority communities, who face additional layers of cultural, societal, and systemic pressure, this conditioning and suppression can be even deeper, making the journey toward self-acceptance and authentic expression more complex and challenging.

As women, we are told how our bodies should look. From advertisements to social media, we are fed an impossible image. An image that seems to change overnight and, with the introduction of filters and AI, is simply not achievable.

In many areas of the world, we are told what we are and are not allowed to wear and what to even do with our bodies. We are hypersexualized from a young age and then shamed for our bodies and our clothes. We're told things like our shoulders are distracting and our skirts are too short.

We are taught to be smaller, thinner, and less. We are taught to hate our bodies and change our bodies. But no one teaches us to love our bodies, or to appreciate, connect to, and honor the body's power.

At least, no one ever taught me that.

I began sucking in my stomach as a child, trying to make sure it always looked flat, like the images I saw on TV. I was uncomfortable when I sat down and my skin would roll over the top of my pants. Perhaps this is where the tension in my abdomen began.

Dismissing Our Pain

Despite comprising half of the world's population, women's bodies have been historically left out of medical research trials, leading to huge gaps in information about our own health. This underrepresentation has not only led to a general misunderstanding of our bodies, but it has led to misdiagnoses and mistreatment as well. Women's pain is often not taken seriously, a disparity that is significantly worse for women of color. Our pain is chalked up to anxiety, or we hear things like "that's normal" when referring to severe menstrual pain. For example, even though almost 10 percent of reproductive-age women suffer with endometriosis, it takes almost 10 years to receive a diagnosis and appropriate medical care for this debilitating disease.

When I began menstruating, I felt only shame and embarrassment at what my body was doing. I tried to hide it every month, making sure no one knew that I was a woman with a healthy and functioning body. And when the pain of my menstruation kept me home from school and became unmanageable, I was put straight on pain killers and eventually birth control, without a single thought that maybe these symptoms were asking to be witnessed, to be seen, or that there was an underlying message. It's no wonder we swallow our pain or push through it, but this is just another example of how we lose the connection to the signals from our own bodies.

Muting Our Voices

As we discussed in Chapter 2, women are not only taught to shrink our bodies and suppress our pain, but we're taught our voices should be soft-spoken as well. There is a huge difference between how we raise boys versus how we raise girls. Boys are encouraged to be loud, to be leaders, to exert their voices. But when girls display these qualities, they are called bossy or aggressive. We see over and over again how survivors of sexual violence are undermined, gaslit, or completely silenced. Women are frequently interrupted or talked over in work environments, and the message is heard loud and clear: We are expected to blend in, be submissive, and be quiet.

This constriction and suppression isn't our natural state. As we explored earlier in the book, we're often handed these early narratives to conform, sit still, be quiet, speak only when we're told, not get our hands or clothes dirty, and the list goes on. We become so squished into ourselves, with these rules taking us out of our bodies, training us to ignore our own cues and even needs, that it feels normal to be disconnected. But our natural state is connection and the freedom to listen to and be in our bodies.

When every word is measured, when everything has to be perfect, and there is no room to make mistakes, to try, or to slow down, the pressure builds inside us. When we feel like we have to control everything and contort ourselves in the process, the body will speak. Next time you notice yourself hiding your authentic self, or monitoring your words, behaviors, and opinions around others in order to keep the peace or maintain the relationship, pay attention to how your body is responding. Are you on guard, careful, and in defense mode? Are you tense or constricted? Where? We shrink or mute ourselves to keep ourselves safe, but what we don't realize is, it comes at a cost.

Our Authentic Self and Survival Responses

We talked a bit about survival mode and fight or flight in the last chapter, but let's take a deeper look at all of the survival responses, and especially the fawn response. Pete Walker, a psychotherapist known for his work on complex trauma and complex PTSD, is often credited with popularizing the term the *fawn response*. The fawn response, or fawning, is a pattern that can develop in response to chronic stress or relational fear, and tends to look like suppressing or people-pleasing behaviors, often in an effort to pacify others and avoid conflict. This can involve suppressing one's own needs, opinions, or emotions in favor of others'. Over time, consistently suppressing our needs or reactions can sometimes show up physically as muscle tension, headaches, or fatigue, because long-term stress keeps the body on high alert.

It's important to recognize the other three primary survival responses as well, since we have experienced each of them at some point. These responses are healthy, automatic, and instinctive strategies our bodies use to protect us in moments of real or perceived danger. This is just an overview and not a comprehensive list.

The Fight Response

The fight response can show up when we confront a threat head on. This reaction may arise as anger, irritability, or a strong urge to defend ourselves. Physically, it can manifest as an increased heart rate, rapid breathing, and muscle tension.

The Flight Response

The flight response drives us to escape or avoid danger. When we enter flight mode, our instinct is to withdraw or flee from the source of threat. Common physical sensations may include feeling restless, shaky, or even dizzy.

The Freeze Response

The freeze response occurs when neither fighting nor fleeing feels possible or safe. In this state, we may become still, or numb, almost as if we are trying to become invisible. This can manifest as feeling frozen, or a sense of being "stuck."

It's essential to understand that survival responses are rarely straightforward or limited to just one reaction. Because we are complex beings, our responses can blend together, shift over time, or vary depending on the situation or trigger.

Research has shown that long-term stress can influence the immune system. In 1994, a man named Dr. Robert Anda enrolled 17,337 adults in a study looking at adverse childhood experiences (ACEs) and the long-term effect on health outcomes. It was a study that looked at 10 categories considered adverse in childhood. The categories included:

- Physical abuse
- Sexual abuse
- Emotional abuse
- Physical neglect
- Emotional neglect
- Household substance abuse
- Household mental illness
- Domestic violence
- Parental separation or divorce
- Incarcerated household member

Since this study was conducted, researchers have expanded the categories to include:

- Racism
- Community violence
- Poverty

The study found correlations between higher ACE scores and increased likelihood of experiences such as:

- Depression
- Suicide attempts
- Heart disease
- Cancer and chronic lung disease
- Obesity and physical inactivity
- Substance abuse disorders

The researchers noted that people with higher ACE scores were more likely to report long-term health difficulties. This is thought to relate to the impact of early stress on the nervous system. This makes sense as these states reflect a nervous system that's working really hard to stay safe.

I want to also note here that whether you score one ACE or no ACEs at all, that doesn't mean your experience wasn't real or impactful. We can so often convince ourselves that what we experienced "wasn't that bad" or we tell ourselves it's not a big deal because others had it worse. Your experiences are valid because you lived them and they impacted you. We are all unique, and how we are shaped by our journey depends on so many things. So, if you find yourself looking at the ACE section and feeling like your story isn't reflected, I invite you to pause and find space to honor your own experience.

This is a heavier chapter, and our history and experiences can bring up so much for us. If you are feeling like you need to pause, it's okay to put the book down and tend to yourself. I also encourage you to seek help from a professional when working through some of your experiences.

I didn't have this scientific understanding about the impacts of prolonged stress, but intuitively I had a knowing that I was chronically stressed, and the suppression of my voice, my needs, and my truth was playing a role in my own body tension and chronic infections. As I continued down my own path of self-discovery and connection, I even began to notice my tension patterns and how I would brace myself around certain people, and within certain environments and situations.

When I focused solely on strict health protocols in my own healing journey without addressing the underlying emotional and spiritual issues, it was like trying to put out a raging fire with a watering can. But these rigid routines were doing more harm than good. Following an inflexible nutritional plan with a perfectionist mindset only kept me in a constant state of stress, leaving my nervous system perpetually on high alert. The anxiety over what sugar might do to my body, or the pressure of always bringing my own food to restaurants, was actually increasing my cortisol levels. Instead of healing, I was just trading one form of stress for another.

The awareness of my own tension patterns in my body began to show that, until I could face what was underneath—the patterns I had been stuck in, the fear, and suppressing and hiding of myself—my symptoms would keep coming back.

The Healing Impact

Dr. Robert Anda's research into early adversity opened the door to understanding how our experiences can leave impressions on the body. Research in this area has grown tremendously, and many experts now recognize that while prolonged stress can certainly influence the body, healing and supportive experiences can create cellular shifts as well.

When I began noticing my tension patterns were evolving into infections, I wanted to understand why, and if I could somehow work with that tension, could I begin to ease into it before it turned into full-blown symptoms?

Turns out, I could.

If we think about the body in this way, as a partner and a messenger showing us what needs our attention in order to facilitate healing, perhaps sensations can be viewed as a language, and tuning in is how we begin to speak that language.

It's important to clarify again that I do not believe we are to blame for our symptoms. Sometimes, illness or discomfort simply happens, and the reasons are not always clear. There are many possible causes for physical health issues. That's why, whenever we notice symptoms, the first and most important step is always to seek medical evaluation.

The connection between mind, body, and soul is real, and taking all of these aspects into account can be an important part of understanding and improving our overall well-being. We've all experienced the mind-body connection in one way or another. Whether it was the stress of cramming for final exams that led to a headache, or the nervous jitters in our stomach before starting a new job, it's hard to dispute the connection is there.

Physical signals can be the body's way of protecting us or simply asking us to slow down. It could be chronic-stress related; it could be overdoing, overworking, overgiving; but the body sends us signals to notice.

For example, when we are overwhelmed with work and life stress and we get a migraine, it's almost like the body is pressing Pause and asking us to literally lie down.

When we slow down, we give ourselves the space to witness what is there.

Our body has the innate ability to heal. Take something minor, like a scrape: We don't really have to do anything; our body handles the repair on its own.

In Bruce Lipton's book *The Biology of Belief,* he discusses how gene expression can be impacted by our environment, including our thoughts and perceptions. Lipton's research highlights the idea that our thoughts, beliefs, and the choices we make can directly influence our body chemistry, down to a cellular level. Healing our beliefs about ourselves, changing our thought patterns and making different choices for ourselves can all have a direct and positive impact on our body and our well-being.

Why Coming Home to Our Body Matters

When I first began to reconnect with my own body, I realized how often I had tried to bypass discomfort, both physical and emotional, by staying in my head, staying busy, or using spiritual tools to try to bypass an experience. I would recite affirmations like "I am beautiful" or "My body knows how to heal," but I didn't actually believe them. I thought that if I could just "rise above" my pain, I would be free.

In many spiritual and even esoteric spaces, the focus seems to be on transcending the body. On opening the third eye, connecting with the universal consciousness, or even accessing and operating from a different dimension. But I am not so sure that's what the human experience is about. I think the real work is about being in our bodies and deepening into ourselves.

I was doing all the practices I thought would help me heal, but real freedom and healing, I discovered, was about coming back to myself and meeting myself exactly as I was. Making space for all of me: my fears, my insecurities, my health as it was, and greeting all of those parts of me with compassion and curiosity. The real freedom and healing were found in embodiment.

The spiritual practice of embodiment involves grounding into our bodies, becoming aware of the sensations and wisdom they hold. It's about being present with ourselves, not striving to be someplace else on our journey. It's viewing our bodies as part of the divine and understanding they hold connection. It's realizing that the parts of us we have been taught to suppress, including our anger, rage, sadness, and grief, are deserving of space and our attention. They are not obstacles on our journey; they are guides.

It's only when we are in connection with our own body, triggers, and activations that our sensitivity becomes that superpower. This is how we begin to understand, like we discussed in Chapter 5, what is ours and what is someone else's. From this place of embodiment is also how we begin to reclaim our own energy by understanding what our bodies are telling us in certain environments and working with it.

Talking to the Body

I can't think of a more important partner in this life than the body you inhabit. It is made up of tens of trillions of cells that are ever changing to support you in this lifetime. One way to create a relationship with your body is by talking to it. We can hold so much within our body, but when you listen it will tell you it's truth. If you have any ailments or pain, or feel you are holding on to anything emotionally or spiritually, ask that part of you what it needs—and trust what comes through for you. Let's look at the practices I use with clients for strengthening that partnership.

Body Scan Meditation

A body scan meditation is a mindfulness practice to begin to bring awareness to the body and any sensations that are arising. The goal is to approach this practice from a judgment-free place of curiosity and begin to create a connection between the mind and the body.

Begin this body scan meditation by finding a quiet and comfortable spot. You can be lying down or in a comfortable seated position. And without judgment, start by simply taking notice of your body.

Start from the top of your head and scan the body, moving slowly with your awareness, as you make your way down past your neck, arms, and belly, over your pelvic area and down your legs until you reach your toes. Notice the flow of your thoughts.

Notice any feelings or sensations that may be present in your body.

Where do you feel them? Perhaps in your belly or in your neck. Just notice. You don't have to give them a story or meaning, just recognize they are there.

Notice what they feel like. Can you give the sensation a word? Perhaps *tension* comes to mind, or *ease* or *flow* or *tight*. Just let yourself find a word for the sensation.

Once you've completed this body scan, try speaking to your body. Ask it: What is it I need to know? What would your body tell you right now, if it could talk?

For this practice, it can help to include a Body Scan Map.

Body Scan Map

This is a technique I use in my intuitive readings with my clients. I draw a simple (very simple—think gingerbread man) outline of the human body, and then I pinpoint where I feel or see things in their body, drawing a line out from that point to add an intuitive note. Try it for yourself along with your body scan meditation.

Instructions

Draw a simple outline of a human body on a blank page (or use the one below). This is your "body map." Use it to visually explore where you feel sensations or intuitive messages in your own body, and then reflect on what your body is wanting you to know.

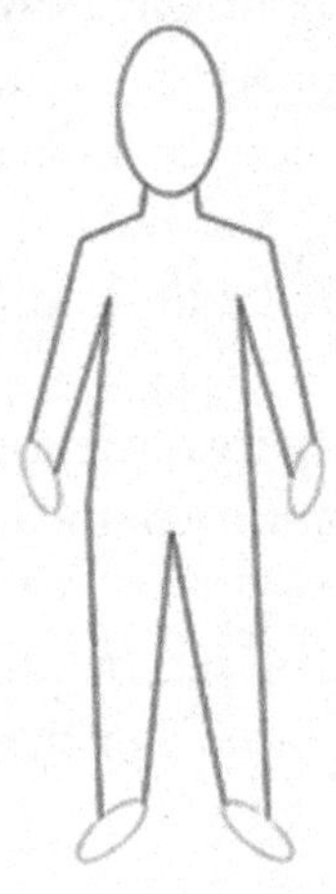

- Use colors, symbols, or words to mark areas where you feel any pain, tension, or discomfort (e.g., red dot on the head for headaches, yellow swirl in the stomach for anxiety).
- Next to each mark, draw a line outward so that you can make an intuitive note next to it.

- Use the body scan meditation to come up with a word for any sensations you feel.
- If it feels right, intuitively explore what your body might be wanting you to know.
- In the margins or around the body, intuitively write messages your body might be sending you. Examples:
    - "I need more rest."
    - "I feel unsafe."
    - "I crave movement."

Practicing the body scan meditation with the Body Scan Map can be a gentle yet powerful way to deepen your own connection with the wisdom of your body. By taking time to notice and honor what arises in us, whether emotions or sensations, we gain a deeper access to our own wisdom. The body is always communicating with us; this practice simply helps us listen more closely. Feel free to revisit your Body Scan Map regularly, noticing how your sensations and messages shift over time. With curiosity and kindness, you are gently building a bridge between your mind and body.

Key Takeaways

As highly sensitive women, we can carry the weight of our experiences, our patterns of perfectionism and people pleasing, and our stories in our bodies. We tense up, we shrink ourselves, we silence our pain, or we overextend. But embodiment invites us to return to ourselves, gently. The body is our very own partner, and reclaiming our relationship to it is part of reclaiming our personal power.

The tension we carry can be a signal, perhaps calling us back to our childhood experiences or other shaping experiences in our lives. But remember, just as adversity can shape us, so too can healing.

Research shows us that our beliefs, our environment, and the choices we make can influence our health at the cellular level. When we choose to listen to our bodies, to honor our sensations, and to offer ourselves compassion, we can begin to shift everything. And I believe this is the true spiritual practice: to honor ourselves and learn to trust ourselves, reclaiming all our parts and our power.

As we move forward to the final wound chapter, it's important to recognize that our disconnection from our own power, sensitivity, and bodies is not just personal; it can be deeply collective and historical. In the next chapter, we'll explore one final source (for this book) of our suppression: the Witch Wound. Together, we'll look at the history of the witch hunts, how fear and control were wielded to silence and diminish women's power, and how the echoes of this wound still shape our lives today. By understanding the roots of this collective trauma, including religion, patriarchy, and the suppression of our own divinity, we can begin to reclaim the gifts and wisdom that have always been our birthright.

✳ 8 ✳

Healing the Witch Wound

Reclaiming Your Divine Power

They told the witches
Be careful what you burn
Or we'll burn you down with it
They force-fed us lies
Packaged as truth,
a poisonous dose
Bred silence from fear
A campaign for our souls
They never imagined
That we'd meet again
Only this time
We'd be holding the flame
We've seen the tactics
Over and over
To keep us distracted

Afraid and divided
Untethered from our souls,
Our hearts, and each other
To snuff out that flame
They'll try every scheme
But they have forgotten
It's only in darkness
That light can be seen

My hair fell long and fiery red around my waist. Next to me was my daughter, her little feet dangling alongside mine. The boat rocked back and forth in a terrifying and lulling manner. Though I didn't know my name, the century, or the location, I knew in the deepest parts of my soul who I was: a healer and a widow who had just been sold into marriage along with my daughter.

The next vision I had was of me running through the woods, fear rising hot inside my stomach. I heard the voices of men and dogs barking off in the distance as they tracked my scent.

I was being hunted.

Clutching a small parcel of dried herbs on the inside of my cloak, I was deep in a forest. I had a knowing that I had prepared a healing remedy for an elderly woman who was suffering in order to ease her pain, but I would never make it there. I was captured and dragged by my hair into a river, held under water, thrashing and writhing to save my own life, but it was useless.

I had drowned.

Gasping and choking for air in my current body, I came out of this past life regression sobbing massive cries that filled my belly and echoed through me, echoing through the centuries, a cry of pain, a cry of being extinguished, and a cry for the daughter I had left behind.

It was a pain and grief so deep and heavy I knew I had been holding on to it for lifetimes.

It made sense in that moment why I was so afraid to say out loud in *this* lifetime that I was a psychic medium—I had tried to walk this unconventional and connected path before, and I was silenced by execution.

So many of us were: the women who worked with the earth and the spirits, the women who healed, the midwives, the oracles. We were feared for our gifts and our magic, but mostly? We were feared for standing in our power.

This is known as the Witch Wound, and the imprint of it is still very much alive in all of us. If you're not familiar, the Witch Wound is a term used to describe the collective trauma imprinted on us from the era of executing people (mostly women, but men as well) for practicing what was considered witchcraft, although the guidelines for what constituted witchcraft were loose. It was a time filled with immense fear and distrust. Your community could turn on you; a neighbor starting a rumor could get you killed. Being too confident, promiscuous, or outspoken could also mean death.

Why am I including the Witch Wound as one of the four wounds discussed in this section of the book? Because even though the witch-hunting times might be history, the act of silencing and controlling women has simply taken on a different shape. It's impossible to talk about the fear of being seen, using our voices, and the disconnection from our own intuitive and spiritual abilities without discussing this wound.

These patterns of shrinking and fear are the echoes of generations who learned that visibility and divine connection could be dangerous. The fear of women and witches generated during those times, and earlier, has been carried through centuries and passed down through generations.

First, let's take a look at this grim history.

The Witch Hunts

When we truly understand how horrific the history of witch hunting was, it begins to make sense that we might collectively carry this trauma and fear our own psychic abilities. Many readers might be most familiar with the Salem witch trials in North America that took place in the late 1600s, but the peak of the witch hunts actually spanned more than 300 years: from about 1450 to 1750. During this time, mass trials and executions occurred across Europe and Colonial America.

The witch hunts primarily targeted women who did not conform to patriarchal expectations or societal norms. These women were often seen as rule-breaking, threatening, or overtly sexual. In reality, they were women who stood in their power, worked with the earth, and provided healing and midwifery.

An estimated 60,000 people were executed for witchcraft during this period, with about 80 percent being women. The Hollywood portrayal of how witches were identified often shows it was based solely on rumors or suspicions. But identifying witches actually played a larger role in political and religious agendas, including land accumulation, power consolidation, and reproductive control.

As Celeste Larsen discusses in her book *Heal the Witch Wound* (I recommend this book if this wound speaks to you), in medieval times women actually enjoyed freedoms to gather together, to earn money, and even to drink in taverns without men present. Women had freedoms to sell their bodies, to be healers, and to be midwives. Villages depended on these women for their skills and knowledge, for healing, and for caring for the sick. However, with the rise of capitalism, these women began to be seen as a threat to the systems, and especially to the men, who could profit from their loss of power, body autonomy, and land. Many scholars, most notably Silvia Federici, claim that the witch hunts were a carefully crafted measure to suppress women and gain control over reproduction in order to reinforce male dominance and capitalist-patriarchal control.

Remember how we discussed fear as a tactic to control? Well, the means by which terror was spread during these times are difficult to read about, so I will spare you the descriptions since, as highly sensitive people, we don't need graphic or gory imagery getting stuck in our minds. But suffice it to say it was brutal at best. It makes sense that this fear, spread across centuries, would still be present in our bodies today.

So, how might this impact us in modern times? Let's take a look.

Were You a Witch?

Some people have vivid memories of being executed for witchcraft in past lives, myself included. As I shared earlier in the book, when I began the deep healing work around sharing my psychic mediumship abilities with the world, I carried an immense amount of fear.

What would people think of me if I said I could speak to the dead?

Surely, they will kick me out of my graduate program if they find out—I'll be categorized as delusional and won't be allowed to work in the field of mental health.

If my parents find out, they will think I am communing with the devil.

These were all thoughts that crossed my mind. The fear ran so deep that when I first said out loud to a loved one that I was a medium, my heart was racing, I started sweating, and I went into a full-blown panic attack.

This was a deep, deep fear.

When I discovered that I had been drowned for being a healer in a past life, it made so much sense why I was terrified to share this truth. And while there were many fears and layers to why I was afraid to publicly acknowledge my ability to speak to the dead, this personal history, this execution for honoring my healing ability and sharing my gifts, could not be ignored as a factor. It made sense that I was scared of my own abilities. I was supposed to fear my magic because the world had feared it for centuries.

Even if you have no recollection of a past life as a healer or witch, or whether you even believe in past lifetimes at all, modern science is exploring how the effects of stressful experiences can echo through generations.

This suggests that the experiences of our ancestors living through fear-driven times may be stored in our biology today, influencing our stress responses, health, emotional patterns, and even expression of ourselves. Some research, including work exploring the descendants of Holocaust survivors, points to the possibility that large-scale, overwhelming events can leave imprints that ripple through generations. Because the witch-hunting time spanned across many cultures and centuries, it is reasonable to consider that many of us might carry some imprint of this history.

Not sure if these times impacted you? Here are some of the commonly accepted manifestations of this wound:

Signs and Symptoms of the Witch Wound

- Difficulty speaking up or using your voice
- Fear of your own spiritual, psychic, or intuitive abilities
- Fear of being seen
- Shrinking yourself or avoiding attention
- Flashbacks or dreams of being drowned, hanged, burned, or executed
- A tightness in your throat when trying to speak
- Suppressing or downplaying your spiritual beliefs for fear of ridicule

It's hard to look at these symptoms without seeing the pattern of self-silencing. This shrinking and censoring of ourselves due to societal pressures and expectations to be pleasing and digestible to others has far-reaching effects, including our professional lives, our tendency to prioritize others above ourselves, and so on.

We may not be executing witches in the town square anymore, but the fear and mistrust of women standing in their power is still around today. Look at what happens to strong, visible women in our modern society. They are held to standards men are not: The things we celebrate in powerful men are vilified in women. We tear women apart for aging; we criticize how they dress; we have opinions on their choice to have children or not have children. Think about the female celebrities we put on pedestals and then tear down. Society still loves to take down powerful women. Look at Martha Stewart, Janet Jackson, or Meghan Markle. Each of these women has faced intense scrutiny and backlash throughout their public careers. Whether it was Martha Stewart's imprisonment for insider trading at the height of her business success, Janet Jackson's criticism after the wardrobe malfunction, or Meghan Markle's relentless media scrutiny as a member of the royal family, these are examples of how women standing in their power are often held to a different standard than men, facing disproportionate criticism. It's hard to ignore the deep-rooted fear society has of powerful women.

Why might that be?

Gender Hierarchy

The Witch Wound is deeply intertwined with patriarchal frameworks and organized religion. It is crucial to understand that this wound stems not only from being hunted for witchcraft, but in a larger framework of the patriarchy. The patriarchy is a system of social, political, and economic structures where men (primarily white, heterosexual men) hold positions of power and authority, often through the oppression of women, LGBTQIA+ individuals, and minorities. It's important to note that the patriarchy is a system issue, it is not interchangeable with individual "men," and men can also experience harm under patriarchal norms such as intense expectations of masculinity and emotional suppression.

The Witch Wound often manifests as a fear of self-expression and empowerment, which are key factors that the patriarchal system uses to suppress and limit women. This continued suppression of women and their connection to their intuition and power can affect how women perceive their own worth, spiritual abilities, and place in the world today.

It's impossible to talk about self-silencing in women without discussing the impact of living within a gender hierarchal system. We are consistently asked, and sometimes forced, to prioritize others and sacrifice our mental, physical, emotional, and spiritual well-being in the service of this system.

Our inheritance of the Witch Wound and continued exposure to systemic gender inequality plays a real role in gender dynamics, and women's access (especially women of color or minority women) to leadership roles, bodily autonomy, and equal opportunities.

As we begin to recognize how the patriarchal framework perpetuates fear and suppression in women, it's also important to consider the deeper spiritual consequences of this system. Throughout history, many institutions, including religious ones, have reinforced the idea that our inner wisdom, spiritual connection, and even life-giving power as women are suspicious or untrustworthy.

Religion and Suppression of Spiritual Abilities

A big part of being able to share my mediumship abilities was untangling myself from my own understanding of divinity and connection, an understanding that had been greatly molded from being raised a strict Roman Catholic. As I understood my own religious teachings, God was separate from me. He (a male being) could be accessed and connected to through the sacraments, which could only be administered by other anointed men. I remember a conversation with my mom when I was a kid in which she was explaining the sacrament of baptism, which in Roman Catholicism initiates a person into the church by cleansing them of original sin. It is considered a necessary passage in order to enter into heaven after death. As a child, I was so perplexed by this, asking my mom, "What about infants who die before being baptized?" It didn't make sense to me that God would cast away the souls of innocent babies simply because they never received a sacrament.

There was a deep belief growing up that I was inherently flawed and sinful, in need of redemption. And that true power and connection was something external, often out of reach, without the help of a more powerful and divinely appointed man.

My understanding was that only religious heads or saints had this direct access to God or angels. Anything outside of that was viewed as paranormal or dangerous, with few miraculous exceptions, of course. I was fully convinced that I needed an exorcism when spirit began visiting me. It did not even dawn on me that I was capable of communicating with angels or spiritual beings. So, I had a lot to unpack about my own beliefs as I went down this path. And naturally, I began to question everything I had been taught about connection to the divine.

One idea the Catholic church rejects is that of reincarnation. We are told that we have just one life to live, and then we are met with judgment in the afterlife. When I began outwardly questioning this belief in my early 20s, I was met with the message that it was dangerous to think that way. I have since untangled from this belief due to my own experiences, past life regression, and general interest and research in the topic.

There have been many case studies that are hard to argue with, but one I find fascinating is the case of James Leininger. If you're not familiar, James was a child who, at the age of two, began having vivid nightmares of plane crashes. He started sharing very specific details of an aircraft carrier, the name of his fellow pilot, and how his aircraft was shot down over the Pacific Ocean. After looking into it, his parents were able to match these details to the life and death of a real pilot, James Huston Jr., whose plane was shot down during combat in WWII. It's a fascinating story with the case being investigated by Dr. Jim Tucker and featured in the book *Soul Survivor.*

Now, I am in no way here to ask you to believe what I believe or question your religion—quite the opposite, actually. The whole objective of this book is about building trust in yourself. Whether or not you subscribe to the idea of reincarnation or personal divinity, I invite you to reflect on this: Many of us are taught through a variety of systems that we are fundamentally flawed, in need of redemption, and not worthy of divine connection without the help of others deemed "more" divine than us. We internalize that there is something inherently wrong or sinful or dangerous about who we are, especially that our bodies or our desires or our spiritual connection is evil. This belief can warp our sense of self, creating a separation from our own consciousness and inner divinity. Instead of seeing ourselves as whole, sacred beings, worthy of connection, we begin to view ourselves as broken, in need of redemption or saving from our own nature. It defuses the very power and ability we are actually born with.

This kind of belief system can also create a deep sense of fear and pressure, often leading us to seek approval and guidance outside of ourselves rather than trusting our own inner wisdom. What might shift for us if we questioned these patriarchal narratives and explored the possibility that we are already whole, and that our journey is about remembering and reconnecting with our true selves?

This idea that we are flawed, sinful, and unworthy of divine connection on our own, combined with the collective experience of the Witch Wound, has helped shape the way generations of women relate to themselves and their own spiritual abilities. Understanding the role that these fears and narratives have played on our own belief in and connection to our power allows us to begin to gradually release beliefs that no longer serve us and create a more empowering belief system.

Normalizing Divine Connection and Psychic Abilities

Intuition is used every day in art, music, writing, and creative endeavors. We can even trace a lot of our modern science and medical breakthroughs back to an intuitive knowing or inner voice. Alexander Fleming credited his discovery of penicillin to his observation of mold and bacteria growing in a petri dish. There was an obvious place where the bacteria were unable to grow, which led him to intuitively question and pursue the possibility that this mold could kill bacteria. Albert Einstein was also well-known for his belief that science and intuition intersected. He even stated that he did not think so much in thoughts, but more images and intuitive insights that came to him spontaneously.

But, while intuition has been openly credited as a source of insight and intellect among male scientists, women who relied on these same abilities for their midwifery or healing were often mocked, or worse, persecuted. As many feminist scholars have noted, this same ability and connection to inner wisdom, often celebrated and praised in men, was declared dangerous in women.

While times have certainly changed, and so many people now accept psychics, mediums, energy healers, and those who work with mystical, esoteric, or spiritual practices, there is still a lot of fear and misunderstanding surrounding these traditions. Since sharing my truth openly that I am a medium, I've been accused of selling my soul to the devil, of demon worship, and more. While it used to bother me, now I have accepted that the folks who see my abilities this way are simply afraid. But intuition and spiritual connection are not mysterious, rare abilities, or anything to fear; they are abilities we all have, and they are especially accessible to highly sensitive women. I bet you have your own story of an unexplained or mystical experience, or several experiences where you knew something without being told, or you heard a voice or saw a spiritual being. What would it feel like to lean in to this part of yourself? To trust in your own inner knowing on a daily basis? To reclaim the beautiful gift of spirit guide connection, angel guidance, ancestor connection, and access to a greater source of wisdom?

Healing the Witch Wound involves not only addressing the personal impacts related to this inherited trauma, but also dismantling the beliefs instilled upon us aimed at keeping us small, obedient, and silent. I want to note here that the patriarchy is a large systemic issue that is embedded across public and private spheres, and not an individual burden to overcome. Religion offers some beautiful and positive teachings and rituals, and it can also uphold some of these patriarchal structures. I still have a very close connection with Jesus and often call upon Mother Mary. My relationship with these divine beings has deepened with my own questioning and reclamation of parts of myself I had buried. You can be deeply religious and spiritual. It's all about keeping your choice at the forefront and finding your deep and inherent worth within. Keeping that in mind, there are some practices that can help you begin to reclaim your voice, intuition, and power and work toward healing this wound within yourself.

Healing Practices

As mentioned in the last chapter, while research shows that inherited trauma can impact our genes, healing can also have lasting intergenerational effects. So how do we heal ourselves from this long history of fear and pain? The first step is a sort of unlearning and reconditioning of what we may have been taught about witches, healers, and even ourselves as women.

What negative stereotypes come up for you when you think of a witch? Is it the classic grotesque moles or green skin? Is it boiling eyes into soup and stealing the youth of children? Maybe it's something demonic and dark. Fear has always been a powerful form of propaganda used to sway the opinions of the public and steer us to move and think a certain way. These images of what it means to be a witch were powerful propaganda, and they worked.

But who were witches, really? They were the healers of the community who worked with nature and understood our connection to something greater. They were strong women who understood their power. They were the midwives equipped to help shepherd souls into this earthly realm. They were the medicine women who held space for their people and communities. Reclaiming these pieces in ourselves and letting them shine through is one way to begin healing this wound.

Many of the following practices, and even throughout this book, are inspired by the wisdom and traditions of Indigenous cultures, who have long recognized the interconnectedness between humans, the spirit world, and the natural environment. Indigenous women, in particular, often served as healers and knowledge keepers, working closely with plants, herbs, and the cycles of nature to support the well-being of their communities.

As you explore the following practices, hold gratitude for those that have preserved and shared these teachings for centuries, often through great adversity.

To Begin Healing the Witch Wound in Yourself

To begin healing the Witch Wound within yourself, start by recognizing how it might be manifesting in your life. Are you afraid of your own spiritual or intuitive abilities? Why? Does your connection to nature or love of herbs and natural remedies feel silly? Why? Are you constantly self-silencing or afraid to speak up? Why? If it feels true for you, let yourself explore what past lives you may have lived. Look at your own ancestral lineage: Where did your family come from? Ask to hear stories about your great-grandmothers and grandmothers and what traditions they held, both publicly and perhaps in secret. I have had so many sessions with women where their ancestors come through explaining that they hid their spiritual abilities out of fear, and they urge their granddaughter or great-granddaughter to embrace her gift, not fear it.

Prompts for reflection on your healing journey:

- **Reclaiming Your Voice:** When have you felt unheard or silenced regarding your own intuitive abilities or mystical experiences? What's holding you back from speaking your truth today?
- **Being Seen:** When have you faced rejection for being yourself or sharing a witchy part of you? What changes would help you express your true self now?

- **Trusting Your Inner Guidance:** Recall when you had a gut feeling about something. What did that knowing feel like? Where did it show up in your body? What does your inner wisdom want you to know now?
- Are you afraid to share your intuitive or spiritual gifts, and do you talk yourself out of them even, convincing yourself they are merely coincidence? Reflect on why that might be.

Envision Yourself from Past Lifetimes

- If you feel a connection to past lives, do you have an intuitive knowing about a specific past life? Who were you? Perhaps a healer, midwife, or oracle? When you close your eyes and tune in, what elements do you see visually from your past? Keep a journal to piece together your visions and knowings.
- What do you intuitively feel you had to endure that you might be carrying still today? Perhaps a physical, emotional, or social pain or challenge?
- How can you use this lifetime to step out of those patterns of fear and into your own power?

Connect with Spirit

Connection with our spirit guides and team of angels is available to each and every one of us, no matter our religion, culture, upbringing, or experiences. Like any other relationship, it's a two-way street and requires daily communication in order to be a strong one.

Try this:

- Sitting in a relaxed and quiet space, first connect with your breath to center your energy. Once you feel grounded, begin by simply letting your spirit team know that you are ready for a deeper connection. You might ask them to introduce themselves. You can do this by speaking out loud or to yourself. Then be patient, and most importantly, trust what comes through.
- You may receive answers in the form of visions or spoken words. Your spirit team may communicate through signs and synchronicities at first, as those are often easiest to spot when starting out. Trust your own experience. Keep a journal to write down and date the messages or intuitive nudges you receive. Each day, come back to this space and continue a dialogue. You can ask questions, seek guidance, or simply tell your spirit team how you're feeling.
- Traditional prayer probably taught you to ask for help or guidance, or even plead for it with statements like "Please help me . . ." Make a shift, and try beginning with "Thank you" instead, such as "Thank you for your guidance on this issue," and see how it feels to communicate in this way.
- You might feel silly at first, but that's because there is a whole lot of conditioning and limiting beliefs driving that feeling. Acknowledge that you feel silly and try anyway.

- In Chapter 10, I will outline some deeper practices for connecting with your own inner wisdom.

Connect with the Earth

Reflect on your relationship with Mother Nature and the natural world around you.

Perhaps you are very connected to the animals, or you keep a garden. Or perhaps you don't really pay much attention to your natural surroundings. If that's the case, what are some ways you can begin to reawaken this connection within yourself?

Some ideas might include:

- Begin a garden or grow herbs in your kitchen.
- Practice earthing by placing your bare feet on the grass or land outside.
- Listen to the breeze or the soothing rustle of the trees.
- Talk to the natural world around you, like the plants and animals.
- Incorporate deeper ethical and sustainable practices into your daily life.
- Begin to pay attention to and honor your own natural cycles.

Embrace Your Spiritual Abilities

We all have access to psychic or intuitive abilities; some people might have an easier time connecting to these than others, but they are gifts available to us all. Get to know yourself and where your strengths lie. In Chapter 5, we touched briefly on two of the Clairs, but I will outline those further for you in Part III of the book, where I also share in-depth practices like journaling, oracle cards, automatic writing, and more, to help strengthen your intuitive abilities.

Before we jump into those practices, one of the best ways to begin reclaiming your power and intuitive gifts is through creating a ritual and a sacred altar space that you can return to time and time again.

Create Your Sacred Space

Decide on where you can perform your daily ritual, uninterrupted. What time works best for you? What materials do you want to include? I always light a candle to signify that my space is open and ready for my practice. I keep my journal and pen nearby and often hold my rose quartz crystal. When I finish, I blow out the candle to signify the closure of this sacred time. Think about what elements you would like to include in your own space. Maybe you love crystals or twinkling lights, the glow of candles, or the energy of fresh flowers or a potted plant. Let yourself play and reconnect with the witch within while creating this magical space for yourself to return to each day.

Set Up an Ancestral Altar

Create an altar for your ancestors, honoring your lineage and their own journeys. I have a dedicated space in my office with photos of my sister, aunts, grandmothers, and great-grandmothers, along with some of the heirlooms I have inherited to remind me of their own strength and journeys. I feel that they are watching over me. What elements can you include to honor your own ancestors?

Set Your Intention

Intentions are gentle and inviting thoughts or statements that set the tone for your practice. You might choose an intention to release what's holding you back or an intention to connect more deeply with your soul's guidance. Whatever you choose for that day, be clear about your needs for the day, stating them aloud or writing them down.

Be Consistent but Flexible

To truly reap the benefits of your daily ritual, commit to showing up for yourself. Make it a practice you return to and look forward to. However, allow for flexibility as well; you don't want this to be an added pressure or stress on you. Life can be unpredictable, and it's okay to adapt your practice to fit your schedule and season of life. Building in days off or adjusting your ritual when necessary is part of the process.

Key Takeaways

The Witch Wound, like each of the core wounds, is simply an invitation for us to witness another part of ourselves. By reclaiming our connection to our inner wisdom, and to both spirit and Mother Nature, we can begin to transmute this inherited wound. The healing of this wound will ripple out to future generations who will no longer fear their own connection and divinity. As you honor your own journey back to yourself and to your spiritual gifts, you are making space for others to also honor their intuition, spiritual connection, and relationship with the earth.

In Reflection

We have just explored four very deep wounds that I believe impact us as highly sensitive women. These are the wounds that have helped shape us and our stories. Some of the stories we inherited might not be the story we want to carry any longer. As we have learned, the only way to make real, lasting change is to shed light into those areas, to gently expose them, and to make space for healing. In doing this, we are able to begin rewriting more empowering stories for ourselves.

As we conclude the second part of this book, I invite you again to pause and reflect on your own journey thus far. What wounds have been driving your own patterns? In what ways can you begin showing yourself compassion for your own experiences? Take a moment to honor where you are in your own journey and recognize the courage and strength it takes to even put eyes on some of these wounds.

What Lies Ahead

As we journey into the final part of this book, we will journey even deeper into the work of healing and creating lasting transformation. I will guide us through the practice of shadow work to gently face what has been hidden and begin releasing some of the limiting beliefs we've uncovered. We'll explore how to consciously choose new stories and ways of moving that align with the life we are creating for ourselves.

In the Ancient Wisdom chapter, you will find practical exercises for developing and strengthening your intuition, as well as how to tell the intuitive voice from fear. Then we move on to reclaiming our voice, the importance of setting healthy boundaries, and redefining who we are in ways that honor us today. This final section of the book is an invitation to step fully into your own power, deciding and clarifying what truly matters to you, and to begin living from an anchored place of wholeness, courage, and self-trust.

Part III

GENTLE RECONNECTION

We have explored so much of what can define who you are, but your wounds are not your story. They were the circumstances you were handed, very often outside of your control. Now, with intention and healing, you get to decide your story.

Moving through these layers, you might experience the ache of grief. Grief for what was lost, years that feel stolen, safety that wasn't available, or for having to hide parts of yourself. Hold your grief tenderly and give it space while knowing you're not alone in it; it can be a common part of coming home to ourselves.

Exposing these core wounds and becoming aware of them is how we begin to choose differently for ourselves. In our awareness we can also witness our strength and capacity for healing. In this final part of the book, I am going to ask you to begin defining for yourself who you really are. This section is designed to be your guide as you move from awareness into courageous action. We can have all the tools and awareness in the world, but without integrating them into our daily lives, not much will change. I will offer tools, practices, and insights that will serve to guide you in reclaiming your voice, power, and intuition. As you journey through these final chapters, take what speaks to you. As always, let your body and your inner wisdom be your guide, showing you what you need.

This part of the book outlines:

- **An Inside Job**—Embracing Your Shadow
- **An Ancient Wisdom**—Learning to Trust Your Own Magic
- **Finding Your Voice**—How to Reclaim Your Power
- **The Framework**—Deciding for Yourself the Path Forward

Each chapter will offer reflections, personal stories, insights, and gentle practices to help you begin the process of reclaiming what has always been yours: your wholeness, your wisdom, and your way back home to yourself.

Let's begin.

9

An Inside Job

Embracing Your Shadow

In the last part of this book, we explored some of our core wounds as highly sensitive people. You will undoubtedly have your own personal past and wounds as well. In this chapter, we are going to lean in to those wounds, making space for them and releasing the limitations they may have created within us.

We often hear phrases like "I would die for you" or "I would kill for you" as the ultimate declaration of how much we love that person. But I believe a truer act of love, for both ourselves and others, is how much we would heal ourselves. How willing are we to look at our own shadow, and pain, to bring it to the surface to be felt? How much of our grief and anger can we witness and sit with? Because it is actually this healing that brings more love and healing into the world, not the violence of murder or sacrificing your own life.

There is a saying that "hurt people hurt people," and maybe that's true. But sometimes, hurt people heal and create safe spaces and softness, impacting generations to come. These people are often called *cycle breakers*.

A cycle breaker is defined as someone who actively works to identify unhealthy patterns in their family history (and often themselves) and works at healing those patterns to intentionally create healthier patterns. And it. Is. Not. Easy. The role of the cycle breaker is so important, but it can be exhausting and isolating. Self-reflection, emotional awareness, and healing can be difficult, but staying stuck in the same cycle is often even harder.

Healing is continuous, and it takes effort. Give yourself a lot of grace, and remember there is no perfect blueprint or timeline; this will look different for everyone. But healing is possible.

It took years of work and self-discovery to identify and explore my own patterns—and there are always more popping up for me to witness and invite in. In this chapter, we'll discuss how everything can be a message and what some of our repeated or stuck emotions might be telling us. I will walk you through three practices that support in creating new neural pathways. And then I share my favorite practice for shadow work. One I used to get through a lot of blocks on my own path to success, including writing and publishing this book.

While I am all for healing ourselves to heal our families and heal the world, as you read through, I want you to focus on how the healing you do within can actually change your own life, how you show up in the world, and how you feel on a day-to-day basis.

What Is Shadow Work?

Shadow work feels like a bit of a buzzword these days. It seems everywhere you turn, especially online, someone is talking about shadow work. I'll be honest, when I first started moving inward and unpacking the stuff I had been keeping hidden, I didn't even realize there was a term for what I was doing.

I'm sure you've heard of the term *shadow work*, but what is it, exactly?

According to Jungian psychology, the shadow self represents the denied aspects of ourselves, the pieces of us we deem unacceptable and often hide for fear of rejection. Shadow work is the act of integrating those parts of us and bringing those pieces forward. The parts of us that feel shame, rage, jealousy, or even simply the parts that we've kept hidden because they don't quite fit in with societal expectations. *Ahem*—like being a medium. They might even be the side of us we once embraced but were ridiculed or bullied for.

When I began connecting more deeply with myself and my truth, waves of anger, fear, confusion, and even grief bubbled to the surface, no longer able to be suppressed. These emotions, though uncomfortable, were simply an invitation to witness what I had been squishing down. How tightly I was holding on to and covering up parts of me I didn't want the world to see, or even myself to see. How long I had been silencing myself and living in constant fear. I had to come face-to-face with myself and begin untangling and questioning how I was living and whether it was truly serving me.

Spoiler: It wasn't. Not anymore.

The experiences, patterns, situations, and circumstances we find ourselves in again and again, along with the feelings, thoughts, and emotions that keep surfacing are clues; they are a message from our souls, showing us where we might need some tenderness, gently nudging us to listen. They usually start unnoticed, but they become more and more apparent until we deal with them and decide to move differently. Our inner world, thoughts, and experiences are often deeply meaningful if we can approach them with curiosity instead of criticism and judgment.

Getting Curious

Shadow work is very much about asking questions to uncover the root of our patterns. Now, it might seem silly to bring up hair when I talk about shadow work, but healing the relationship with my hair was one of the first invitations into my own awakening. I remember sitting and calculating exactly how much time of my *one* life I had dedicated to straightening my hair, blowing it out, paying for keratin treatments, avoiding pools, or strategically making sure to never get stuck in the rain for fear that someone would see my hair was actually curly, not straight. All this just to conform to a beauty standard that I didn't fit into. I finally asked the question, *Why? Why am I doing this? Why am I changing myself?* Yes, there is a lot of societal conditioning telling us to look a certain way in order to be accepted, but the deeper pattern for me was about hiding and changing myself to be accepted. As I unpacked that box, there was a Mary Poppins–style unloading of shadow that followed it.

Take a moment to reflect on your life. What are the patterns or habits you're doing on autopilot? Are they truly aligned with who you are? What would happen if you asked, "Why am I doing this?" Maybe the harder question is, "Who am I, really, underneath all the programming and limiting beliefs?"

It's a big question.

I remember very vividly asking myself this question after my daughter was born: *Who am I?* It was like the veil had lifted, like the portal I crossed through into motherhood was showing me truths, magnified. I would look at photos of me and genuinely not recognize myself. I started to unpack all the ways I had been abandoning myself, trying to please others, trying to control everything around me, and just trying to show up as who I thought I was supposed to be. It felt like everything I had ever done was a performance.

What do I like?

Who even am I?

The spiritual awakening journey feels incomplete without this age-old question. It's a question that has been asked since the dawn of time, but I didn't know it would feel like such an identity crisis. We'll go deeper into our identities in Chapter 11.

But as we've been discussing throughout the book, one thing is for sure: We cannot hack our way through. If we try to bypass our inner world or silence our pain and anger, it becomes like a game of Whac-A-Mole where the more we try to squish it down, the more it will find a different way out.

I had refused to acknowledge that I was a medium; I couldn't even bring myself to say it out loud. This was a truth, a piece of myself that I had completely disowned out of fear. This is a shadow. But our shadows don't necessarily have to be negative. Remember how we talked about the difficulty of experiencing or expressing joy? That was a part of myself I had also repressed, unable to give it space.

We all walk through life with so many wounds. We're human; it's part of the growing and learning experience. These wounds can leave imprints, and sometimes those imprints become parts of ourselves we hide or overlook. It's not something separate from us, or even something we are trying to get rid of. It's looking in the mirror at all our imprints and recognizing they are a part of us, but they do not define us.

The Goo

Very often we are not aware of our wounds or our shadow until they begin to wreak havoc on our lives, or until some big life moment pulls us inward, shining a light so we begin to see. As we talked about earlier in the book, there is often a catalyst, something that propels us to notice we need to make changes for ourselves. Those big moments become initiations into transformation, pulling us out of our "safe," autopilot (but out-of-alignment) way of living.

Perhaps a toxic job or relationship startled you into asking the question, "How did I get here?" Maybe it was a serious health diagnosis, a divorce, a near-death experience, a betrayal, or a milestone like the kids leaving for college. All of these big life moments can propel us to ask questions we never asked before.

These deeply transformative times, when filled with intense inner turmoil, doubt, and questioning, are often referred to as a dark night of the soul—a period that can feel like an existential crisis. I don't like to refer to it as a dark night; it sounds so doom and gloom. I prefer to call it the Goo stage, as it is a deeply transformative period and resembles the phase when the caterpillar dissolves into a goo in order to transform and grow into something it didn't even realize was possible. It's also a time when the illusions we've held of ourselves and the world around us begin to dissolve, and we are faced with our true selves.

I also like this analogy because, leading up to this cocoon phase, a caterpillar will become increasingly restless, which is very reminiscent of our own awakening experiences. There is usually a period of restlessness where things seem extra difficult, or we feel like we are climbing an uphill battle; we know things aren't working the way they used to, but we don't really know what to do. The universe is showing us that the path we're on is not it—it's not aligned, and we need to make some changes.

During this transformation, our priorities often completely shift, and we start searching for a deeper meaning or purpose. It can feel like everything is crumbling as we meet ourselves for the first time and we shed layers and layers of conditioning and expectations, allowing ourselves to transform into a truer version of us. This can often feel isolating. As we change, our relationships may shift or even fall apart. Not everyone will understand what we're going through, and not everyone will be growing and changing along with us, and that can be a lonely experience.

The journey of sharing my own truth wasn't just me casually saying, "Oh, yeah, I can speak to spirit," and moving on with my life. The process of unpacking it, along with all the other stuff that was in that box, was a really long and sometimes very difficult process. But looking back, I would do it again because the other side has meant freedom, alignment with myself, and an inner trust in ways I never thought would be possible.

From my own experience, and in working with women going through transformation, I've noticed that something else seems to happen to us in this phase. It's as if we cross an invisible threshold. Our priorities have totally shifted; we have reevaluated our lifestyle choices and our values and what we want out of life, and there's almost this soul knowing that we are now truly moving forward and walking more in alignment with ourselves. And once we cross that threshold, we realize that we can't go back to the way things were or to how we perceived things before. It can be both a liberating and scary feeling.

Peeling ourselves away from what we know, what we're comfortable with, and rebuilding toward something better is not easy, but I believe the rewards are worth the discomfort. True self-discovery and growth require a commitment to exploring our inner depths. To help you begin to explore your own shadows, I've included a reflective shadow work practice at the end of this chapter, as well as other practices to empower you on your own journey.

Shadow work might leave you feeling a bit raw or tender. The realization that we've been self-sabotaging or even abandoning ourselves can feel heavy. We might feel like we've "lost" time or made huge mistakes along the way. And even though we recognize that we don't want to go back, we might also feel a nostalgia or even grief for how things were before. Sometimes, our own autopilot can feel like it was easier, especially when we're elbow deep in transformation. Remember that self-discovery, growth, and change are beautiful, and it's okay to hold and process your feelings for what you are going through and the grief that is coming up.

Life Speaks to Us if We Listen

Life is always communicating with us. The emotions we feel, the physical sensations in our body, the energy we experience around us, the stranger on the street who gets under our skin—it can all be a message. It boils down to tuning in and listening.

My body knew I was living out of alignment long before I did. It signaled when I was in the wrong spaces, consuming things that didn't serve me, and when I was completely abandoning myself. Emotions like envy toward others who stood powerful in their spiritual abilities and expression were just clues, messengers for me to explore what was also possible for me.

What is our body signaling? What would our anger tell us if we let it in and just listened? What would our frustration, resentment, jealousy, or shame want us to know if we gave them space to speak? These emotions aren't bad; they're clues.

- Maybe you feel off or heavy energy because your soul is calling you to move one way, and you're resisting.
- Maybe you feel drained or fatigued because your body is asking you not to be in the environments you keep putting yourself in.
- Maybe you feel jittery because you keep abandoning yourself to keep others comfortable.
- Maybe your inability to rest is tied to how you were raised.
- Maybe you are resentful because you don't know how to ask for what you want and need.

Our internal energy, the emotions we feel, and our physical bodies, just like our intuition, are powerful guides. Shutting down that guide without listening is only doing us a disservice. I would invite you to explore your own feelings and emotions. Do you have a recurring feeling or pattern that you keep noticing in yourself? Maybe it's resentment toward your partner or anger around your mother-in-law. What might these feelings be trying to show you?

Use page 174 or your own journal to reflect on what your own feelings or emotions might be signaling to you.

EMOTION	WHAT MIGHT IT BE SHOWING YOU?
Anger	
Shame	
Grief	
Resentment	
Fear	
Loneliness	
Envy	
Guilt	
Hopelessness	

Understanding our own "stuff" and recognizing our own triggers allows us to begin to unearth the message from our inner wisdom, spirit team, or even the energy around us with much more clarity and ease. Which brings me back to our baseline energy.

Earlier in the book, we discussed our baseline energy, or our core state of being, and how tuning in to ourselves throughout the day can help us become aware of what throws us out of balance, as well as improve our ability to differentiate between our own energy and what belongs to others.

Shadow work helps us to recognize what keeps throwing off our energy so we can acknowledge it without staying stuck. It's about developing the skills to navigate that lake when the ripples turn to waves, whether they're caused by external circumstances or internal struggles.

I want to also mention that taking care of our internal or baseline energy is going to have a lot to do with the boundaries we have in place for ourselves, which we will get more into in Chapter 11.

Owning Our Healing

Shadow work and moving inward to witness pieces of us we've kept hidden can be challenging. Uncovering truths about ourselves or emotions we've buried is difficult. Understanding ourselves—the good, the bad, and the ugly—is challenging! Have you ever heard the saying, "What happened to you wasn't your fault, but it is your responsibility to heal"? Gosh, that's a really hard thing to hear when we are hurting, and there is truth to it. Very often the things that happened to us had nothing to do with us: The pain, the circumstances we were dealt, the burdens that we were forced to carry, they were not our fault.

I know it is a popular thought in New Age spirituality that we have soul contracts, and we signed up to have certain relationships, experiences, and challenges in this lifetime to learn and grow from. It's a fascinating theory, one I find interesting, but I am not sure I subscribe to it. I believe we come to Earth to grow and learn, and our soul grows because of our experiences, yes, but the truth as I see it is we just don't know why things happen. And when you are going through an extremely painful experience, the idea that you chose this experience can be harmful and invalidating and perpetuate the shame you may already feel. Perhaps my views on this will change, but I believe that, as humans, we just don't know why things happen. With that said, if the idea of soul contracts feels empowering to you, embrace that! And if it doesn't, then it's not your truth, and that's okay too.

One thing that is true, though, is that whatever happened to us along the way, we can learn to heal and care for ourselves in the best way we can. For a long time, I tried to break loose from my own pain and past. It felt like an anchor I was dragging behind me, and I wanted to offload it. But I could never seem to break the chains. I have come to understand that it's all a part of me. It's what has brought me to the work I do today. There may not be a way to release the anchor, but I have found that our practices of connection and honoring ourselves become like a sidecar where we can put that weight so it doesn't feel so heavy or keep us stuck. It comes with us, but it does not hold us back anymore. Because our experiences are a part of us, but we are so much more. By holding on to our pain, or replaying it over and over, we allow it to define who we are. It's possible to write yourself a new story and carve a path forward.

Reclaiming Ourselves

Whatever our past or patterns might be, our brains are capable of forming new patterns of thought. This is known as neuroplasticity, the brain's ability to adapt and even completely reorganize its structure, creating new neural pathways. Our thoughts, especially the critical and catastrophizing ones that have become our story, carve a pathway that's well-worn, like a deeply etched groove in a piece of wood. Creating a new groove (or a different way of thinking) in the wood takes time. It's easy to slip right back into that deeply etched groove because it's well-established, and deep. It might feel unfamiliar at first, but with gentler thoughts and different choices, that new groove will become more and more defined.

There are many practices out there that can help us to rewire our brains and create new neural pathways. I am going to be sharing three with you here that are part of my own daily routine, and these are the ones I recommend most to clients: gratitude, mindfulness, and movement.

Gratitude

One of the easiest proven ways to begin creating new thoughts and neural pathways is through a gratitude practice. We touched on gratitude earlier in the book when I shared how, for a long time, I used my gratitude practice to suppress feelings of anger and grief—we're not going to do that! An empowering gratitude practice allows space for all emotions, not just the "positive" ones. It incorporates self-compassion alongside gratitude and encourages us to focus on authentic appreciation rather than forced positivity. You can be immensely thankful for your home, your children, and your health while also creating space for the aches in your heart. You can experience anger, sadness, or grief while still appreciating your best friend, your dog, or the food on your table. It's not about saying, "I feel sad; let me think about something happy."

It's not an either/or at all! It's a tapestry of it all, woven together to create our human experience.

Research has shown that a consistent gratitude practice can actually lead to lasting changes in thought patterns and emotional response. The most common gratitude practices usually call for you to list out at least three things you are grateful for every day. It sounds simple, but this act of focusing on appreciation can help us begin to create new neural pathways in our brains.

In your gratitude practice, focus on honest appreciation for what you already have. This could be simple things like hot, running water or a bed to sleep in; it doesn't have to be extravagant. And if even that feels too difficult or forced, perhaps simply thank yourself. Show gratitude toward yourself for getting you this far. Thank yourself for your will to heal. Thank your body for working so hard to support and care for you.

Deb Dana, a clinician and author specializing in polyvagal theory and trauma treatment, coined the term *glimmers*, which refer to small moments of ventral energy, ease, and connection that surround us daily. Glimmers are not a form of toxic positivity. They're not about dismissing the difficult and simply "looking for the good!" What we want to do is recognize that both of them can exist. We can notice hardship, *and* we can notice moments of connection, regulation, and joy. So how do we know if we've experienced a glimmer? Same as with something that triggers us, as we discussed above: We notice the sensation in our body, and we notice our thoughts. For example: Perhaps it was a little bird who flew to your window and made you smile, or the stranger who held the door for you. It can be any moment in your day that might bring you joy or simply a sense of peace or ease. So, if a gratitude practice feels like too much right now, perhaps start with a glimmer practice.

Here's how you can integrate gratitude into your daily life:

Practical Steps to Cultivate Gratitude

- **Daily Gratitude**: In your journal, write down at least three things you are grateful for each day. These can be simple things, like running hot water, a comfortable bed, or even the sunshine. The act of focusing on your appreciation of these helps shift your mindset and strengthens positive neural connections. I like to shift into appreciation throughout my day by asking, "How lucky am I?" followed by answers like "to have running water" or "to have a cozy bed to sleep in."

- **Appreciation**: Focus on what you already have, grounding into the small comforts and blessings in your daily life.
- **Acknowledge Yourself**: If gratitude feels difficult or forced, start by thanking and acknowledging yourself. Acknowledge your effort to heal and grow. Thank your body for working hard to take care of you, and thank yourself for persevering through challenges.
- **Glimmers**: Notice moments of goodness and ease throughout your day, whether it's a moment in nature or a feeling of quiet peace. Reflect on these experiences with appreciation.

Reflection Exercise: Show up to your gratitude practice each day with curiosity and openness. Use your journal to write down your list of three things you're grateful for or any reflections that arise during your practice. Pause throughout your day to remind yourself, "How lucky am I?"

Mindfulness

A regular mindfulness practice has been proven to change both brain function and structure. Dr. Jon Kabat-Zinn, the founder of mindfulness-based stress reduction (MBSR) describes mindfulness as "paying attention, on purpose, in the present moment, non-judgmentally." This focused attention activates areas of the brain involved in emotional regulation and can help create new pathways for managing both emotions and stress.

Mindfulness can be practiced in various ways, from formal meditation to your everyday activities. A mindfulness meditation practice can be as simple as focusing your attention on the breath, like paying attention to the sensations of the breath in the body or noticing the rise and fall of the belly, or even just the sensation of air as it moves through your nostrils. Mindfulness practices can be brought to anything that we do throughout our day. I often try to apply mindfulness to my meals or cooking, focusing my attention on the ingredients I use, the savory or sweet smells, the sting of onion when I breathe it in, the sizzling of oil in the pot. When eating, mindfulness is all about engaging the senses. Letting the food sit on your tongue, feeling the texture, noticing the flavor. This practice really brings us into the present moment. Here are a few ideas to get you started:

Practical Steps to Cultivate Mindfulness

- **Breath Awareness**: Focus your attention on the sensations of breathing, noticing the rise and fall of your belly or the air moving through your nostrils.
- **Start Small**: Begin with short, two-minute sessions of focused attention on your breath.
- **Present-Moment Focus**: Bring mindful awareness to any daily activity, such as walking, cleaning, or listening to music. Dedicate screen-free time and put your phone away. If you're used to multitasking, try to commit to simply single tasking to create more presence.

- **Nonjudgmental Awareness**: Observe thoughts and feelings without criticism, gently returning focus to the present moment.

Reflection Exercise: Prepare your favorite meal mindfully, staying present from preparation to consumption. Incorporate mindfulness into routine activities like brushing your teeth or washing dishes. Use your journal to note any observations or feelings that arise during this practice.

Remember, mindfulness is not about achieving a particular state, but about cultivating awareness and presence in your daily life. This practice can enhance your ability to manage stress, regulate emotions, and foster a deeper connection with yourself and your experiences.

Movement

We've all heard that exercise can improve your mood, but did you know that it can actually help in the creation of new neural pathways in the brain? I experienced this firsthand when I took up running. I was just on a general journey of getting healthier, but I noticed that running every day became pivotal to my mental health. It's a practice I still do today, 20 years later.

Dr. Wendy Suzuki, PhD, is a professor of neural science and psychology at NYU and a leader in the space of how movement impacts neural pathways. Her research suggests that regular physical activity can support healthier brain function by increasing blood flow, oxygenation, and even help the brain strengthen its neural connections.

Practical Steps for Mindful Movement

Building on Dr. Wendy Suzuki's research and the mindful awareness practices of Dr. Jon Kabat-Zinn, here are some ways you can incorporate gentle and mindful movements into your day to support neuroplasticity and overall well-being:

- **Gentle Movements**: Take a mindful walk or practice gentle and intuitive movements. This isn't about intense workouts like "leg day" or marathon training but about moving with curiosity and awareness.
- **Focus on Awareness**: Pay attention to your body as you move. Notice your breath, the sensations in your muscles, and how your body feels in your space. For example:
  - During a walk, really feel the ground beneath your feet.
  - While stretching, observe areas of tightness or ease.
  - Ask yourself, "How am I feeling today?" and really feel the body.
- **Mindful Observation**: Be open to any physical sensations that arise, whether they create ease or discomfort, and refrain from attaching a story or judgment to them. Simply notice and stay present.
- **Body-Mind Connection**: Recognize how body posture impacts how you feel. For instance:
  - Hunched shoulders and tension may signal stress to the brain.
  - Stretching and sitting tall can communicate more calmness and safety to your brain. Try it for yourself and notice the difference.

- **Modify**: If physical movement isn't available to you, can you focus on the movement of your breath or visualize gentle movements in your mind's eye? This still supports the mind-body connection.

Reflection Exercise: Show up to your movement practice with curiosity and in a way that honors your body. Use your journal to jot down any insights, feelings, or observations that arise during your practice.

Bonus Tip: There is no place more powerful than the present moment. Use your mindfulness time to connect with your inner wisdom or spirit team. Invite them in and start a dialogue. Creating space through mindfulness can help you access inner guidance and clarity.

Gratitude, mindfulness, and movement can open up new pathways within us, supporting healing and deeper alignment. These practices can help us thrive and can support us as we move inward and explore some of our shadows. Now that we've discussed these supportive practices, let's look at an integrative exercise for releasing some of those limiting stories and calling forward more empowering stories.

Shadow Work Practices

So much of what we believe about ourselves might not even be true. It's a story we've been given, or one we created ourselves, and we operate from this limiting place. When we want to level up or create a different way of living for ourselves, these stories can often become the barrier. The first step to changing your story is to become aware of it. Then we can choose to respond from a conscious place. The awareness of critical narratives, fear beliefs, and tired stories acts as a filter, allowing more supportive thoughts and responses through.

In this section, we are going to be honest about what's no longer working in our lives, coming from a supportive place. Remembering that all our patterns and coping mechanisms were there to protect us and served a purpose; they are just not serving us anymore. Exploring our inner world and the pieces of us we've repressed can be difficult work. This is not the time to go full steam ahead. Move gently as you build your capacity to sit with yourself. Create a supportive and nurturing environment for yourself and take breaks. It's not a race.

Before You Start: Create a Calming Environment

- Light a candle, play soft music, and breathe deeply. Invite your spirit team to join you. Keep a journal to connect with your intuitive voice and to use in the writing portion of this exercise.
- Leave judgments behind. Be a safe space for yourself and let your thoughts flow freely.
- Take your time. Don't rush; give yourself the space to process and reflect. This is not a race.
- Tune in to your body's cues. What sensations arise as you explore your thoughts and feelings? Notice them, and if it feels supportive, write them down.
- Trust yourself. Allow your thoughts to emerge without trying to direct them. Trust that what comes up is what you need to focus on right now.

Identifying the Root of the Shadow

You can do this exercise for anything that feels like a limiting belief or story, but for the purpose of this book, we are going to break it down into the Four Wounds: Sensitivity, Connection, Body, and Witch.

In your journal, at the top of the page, start with Sensitivity and draw a line down the center of the page. Then do the same on another page for Connection, for Body, and for Witch.

Sensitivity

Starting with Sensitivity, on the left-hand side of the page, list out all the memories or beliefs you have held about your own sensitivity. Think back to phrases your caregivers might have repeated like "You're so dramatic!" or "You cry over everything!" Reflect on your core beliefs about sensitivity. Do you see it as a weakness or flaw? Do you often try to toughen up? What specific memories come up when you think of your own sensitivity?

Some ideas to get you started:

- **Feeling Shamed for Sensitivity:** Reflect on a time when you were shamed or dismissed for feeling others' emotions or sensing the energy of a space.
- **Pushing Beyond Your Capacity:** Explore moments when you felt you had to push yourself to be more extroverted or outgoing than felt natural. What fears or beliefs drove you to override your own limits?

- **Oversocializing:** Think about instances where you over-socialized or ignored your need for solitude or energy recharge.
- **People Pleasing:** Consider the ways you tend to people-please or prioritize others' needs over your own.

For example, you might write, "When my sister took my teddy bear and I burst into tears, my mom looked over and told me to stop being so dramatic." Sit with this wound for a while and list out as many things as come to mind. When you feel like you've hit a block and nothing else is coming up, take a little break or move on to the next wound.

Connection

Moving onto Connection, on the left-hand side of the page, list out all the memories or beliefs that may have shaped your connection with your own mind, body, and spirit. Think back to phrases your caregivers might have repeated, like "Oh, you're resting again?" or "Susie loves to sing, but she can't carry a tune." Reflect on what core beliefs you've internalized about rest, urgency, or expressing yourself. What are you most afraid of? Why? What specific memories come up when you reflect on feeling safe?

Some ideas to get you started:

- **Fear of Downtime:** Reflect on times when you've felt afraid to rest or labeled yourself as "lazy" for needing downtime.

- **Urgency and Chronic Stress:** Consider the moments when you feel a constant sense of urgency or chronic stress. Where do you think this pressure comes from?
- **Disconnection from Mind, Body, or Spirit:** Identify ways you have disconnected from your own mind, body, or spirit. What situations or emotions might have led to this disconnection?
- **Joy and Relaxation:** Explore why you might not feel safe expressing joy or allowing yourself to fully relax. Are there memories or messages from your past that taught you joy or relaxation were unsafe or undeserved?

For example, you might write, "When my dad walked into the room, I always felt like I needed to look busy." Sit with this wound for a while and list out as many things as come to mind. When you feel like you've hit a block and nothing else is coming up, take a little break or move on to the next wound.

Body

Moving on to the Body, on the left-hand side of the page, list out all the memories or beliefs that may have shaped your relationship with your body. Think back to phrases your caregivers might have repeated, like "We have to walk off that cake we ate!" or "You can't be in that much pain." Reflect on what core beliefs you've internalized about your body, your appearance, and your worth related to it. What limiting stories have become your story? What specific memories come up when you reflect on your physical body?

Some ideas to get you started:

- **Comments About Your Appearance:** Reflect on specific comments others have made about your appearance. How did these words affect your self-image and relationship with your body?
- **Not Good Enough:** Explore times when you felt your body, or your appearance, wasn't good enough. Where do these feelings originate?
- **Diet Culture and Body Image:** Consider the influence of diet culture in your life. What beliefs about food, weight, or body shape have you internalized?
- **Bypassing Your Body's Wisdom:** Recall moments when you ignored or bypassed your body's needs or intuition to make someone else comfortable.
- **Birth Story:** If you have experienced a challenging birth, either your own birth, or in birthing new life, reflect on how this may have affected your relationship with your body.
- **Difficult Physical Experiences:** Think about any physical challenges you have experienced. This could be a car accident, illness, or any experience that impacted you physically. How has this shaped your connection to your body?

For example, you might write, "My mom often took food out of my hands to stop me from eating." Sit with this wound for a while and list out as many things as come to mind. When you feel like you've hit a block and nothing else is coming up, take a little break or move on to the next wound.

Witch

Moving on to the Witch Wound, on the left-hand side of the page, list out all the memories or beliefs that may have shaped your relationship with divine connection and your own spiritual gifts. Think back to phrases your caregivers might have repeated, like "Women can't do that" or "Don't say things like that; we don't believe in that stuff." Reflect on what core beliefs you've internalized about your own divine connection, your gifts, or what it means to be a powerful woman. What limiting stories have become your story? What specific memories come up when you reflect on this wound?

Some ideas to get you started:

- **Loss of Agency:** Reflect on a time when you felt your personal power was taken away. Who or what contributed to this experience, and how has it shaped your beliefs about your own power and autonomy?
- **Fear of Using Your Voice:** Explore the reasons you might be afraid to use your voice or speak your truth. What memories or messages from your past contribute to this fear?
- **Fear of Being Seen:** Consider whether you are afraid to be seen for who you truly are. What are the roots of this fear?

- **Fear Around Psychic Abilities:** Reflect on where your fear or discomfort with your own psychic abilities began. Were there specific events, teachings, or influences that made you doubt, suppress, or fear these gifts?
- **Systemic Conditioning:** Examine what religious, patriarchal, or other systemic beliefs you have internalized as truths about yourself and your own divine connection and power. How have these beliefs shaped your spiritual path, self-image, or relationship with your power?

For example, you might write, "When I shared the experience of seeing an angel, my mom said it was my imagination." Sit with this wound for a while and list out as many things as come to mind. When you feel like you've hit a block and nothing else is coming up, perhaps take a walk or get some movement in to give yourself a break.

Untangling from Limiting Beliefs

After you've created your list, make sure you are in a cozy and supportive space and sit with it. Now go through each line, one by one, and ask yourself, "Is this story my truth? What evidence do I have that supports or contradicts this belief? How might this belief be limiting me?"

Perhaps say each one out loud or to yourself, followed by the statement, "This is not my truth." As you do this, hold compassion for the version of yourself that did the best she could to keep you safe and loved with what she knew at the time. Then release this story. Say out loud, "This is not my story," and let it fall away from you and your energetic field.

Rewriting Your Story

You know how they say, "History is written by the victors"? Meaning the winners of conflict have the power to shape the historical narrative and view, right? Well, you are the victor in your story, and I want you to write the narrative, the one that honors you.

After you have determined that those old narratives are not your truth, one by one, cross them out, and next to each, write a new, more supportive and empowering story. For example:

Old version: "When my sister took my teddy bear and I burst into tears, my mom looked over and told me to stop being so dramatic."

New version: "My sensitivity is a gift, and my feelings matter."

Do this for each of the lines you wrote under each of the wounds. As you cross out each one, you may also want to use the cord-cutting visualization from Chapter 5. Imagine the old narrative as a cord of light, and when you cut that cord, you are releasing it from your energy.

Align with Your New Story and Begin Moving Differently

Review your new stories each day, or as needed, say them out loud and call them into your awareness, aligning with this new energy. Write your new stories down on a note card that you keep on your nightstand or your bathroom mirror. This is an ongoing process. As you move forward, you will come up against more layers of limiting beliefs and old stories. Repeat this process as needed.

Key Takeaways

Remember, moving inward and exploring our shadow side can be difficult work. It's not about finding what's "wrong" with us and erasing it; it's about having compassion for every part of who we are. We get to hold ourselves and honor our paths while also choosing to move differently and create kinder beliefs. Remember, neuroplasticity shows us that we aren't stuck in our stories; we can create these gentler pathways in our brains.

As you close this chapter, connect with your breath and body. Honor the courage that it takes to explore your more challenging parts and past. As you continue on your journey, be patient with yourself and celebrate how far you've already come.

As we journey on to the next chapter, I want you to remember your own magic. Each of our souls carries an ancient wisdom, one that stretches beyond this lifetime and location. It's a knowing that continues to guide us toward our truest path. In the next chapter, we'll explore what inner wisdom is, how to reconnect with it, and some common obstacles that get in the way. Through eight intuitive practices that I recommend to clients and use myself, I will guide you to strengthen the sacred connection between your body and your heart's deepest callings.

10

An Ancient Wisdom

Learning to Trust Your Own Magic

The Journey Back to Yourself

We've all experienced moments of profound connection to our inner wisdom. Maybe it was the first time you met your spouse and you thought, "I'm going to marry this person," or perhaps you were hugging Grandma good-bye, and something told you this would be the last time you saw her. Whatever it was, it was an undeniable inner knowing that you didn't even question; you just knew.

After reading this book, this is what I want *most* for you. I want you to be able to trust in yourself so deeply—to trust in your inner voice, your needs, your body—that you don't have to question it or prepare logical research to back it up, or phone a friend to make sure you're not crazy. Trust yourself so deeply that you don't even think about it.

Learning to trust ourselves is key to breaking free from perfectionism, people pleasing, and self-doubt. It allows us to cultivate confidence in ourselves and shift out of uncertainty and into clarity.

Learning to trust myself was the hardest and greatest gift I gave myself. For so long I doubted my own experiences as a medium, chalking them up to coincidence, or worse, telling myself I was crazy. I didn't want to believe in my own power. Maybe I thought it would change my life too much, and I just wasn't ready.

Developing your psychic abilities, your intuition, or your mediumship is all about learning to trust yourself. Trust what you feel, see, and hear, and build confidence to say those things out loud to other people. Now, as I'm sure you gathered so far, I wasn't in the business of telling people about my supernatural experiences. The floating faces in my bedroom and disembodied voices were just never a topic I brought up over coffee with friends. But I slowly built a deeper trust in my own experiences, and in turn, myself, and that foundation allowed me to reclaim and share parts of myself without fear.

As you read through this chapter, keep an open mind and heart. Remember, you already have access to all the wisdom within; you are just remembering how to hear it and to begin trusting it.

What Is Inner Wisdom?

Let's start with defining what our inner wisdom even is. While we often refer to it as a "voice," it can also be an intuitive understanding or knowledge from a place deep within us. This wisdom can manifest in many ways, so don't be discouraged if you don't hear an actual voice. Sometimes it's more of a physical or gut feeling.

Intuition is our built-in navigation system, a gift we all possess as humans. I believe it's our higher self or universal knowledge designed to keep us on track and guide us toward our highest good. We're all born with intuitive abilities, though they may present differently for each individual.

The intuitive voice will very often emerge as:

- Calm and grounded
- A subtle idea popping in and out of our awareness
- Not harsh or judgmental
- A strong sense of knowing without a logical explanation
- A gentle pull, guiding us from a place of energy in the body
- An expansive or light feeling in the body
- Sensations like goosebumps or butterflies

You might notice yourself saying "this just feels right" or "I don't know how I know, but I just know." Sometimes it will feel like a pull toward something.

Research on mind-body connection shows that our bodies play a major role in how we sense, interpret, and respond to the world. While we often think our brains are in control, sending information from the top down, our bodies actually process much of our lived experience first. This is why I believe in order to build a relationship with our inner wisdom, we have to be connecting with our physical bodies as well.

Think about any of the Clair senses: clear seeing, clear hearing, clear feeling, clear knowing, they all come through the senses of the body. Intuition and the physical sensations go hand in hand.

While our gut feelings and intuitive voices are often communicating with us, it's important to recognize that not every thought or feeling is coming from our inner wisdom. Sometimes what we consider to be our inner wisdom is actually our fear, anxiety, or a ruminating thought. Understanding the difference between the two is critical for making empowered decisions. And don't worry, with practice you will be able to tell the difference.

Fear vs. Intuition

One of the top questions I receive as a psychic medium is "How do I know if it's my intuition or my anxiety?" And, believe me, I get it! Our fears can be loud; we have so much to worry about, and those thoughts can get in the way, clouding our ability to truly tap into our intuition.

The key to identifying your inner wisdom is understanding that it differs from your critical inner voice, inherited narratives, or personal fears. By becoming familiar with how these other voices manifest (which we've been doing throughout the course of this book), you can begin to distinguish your intuition from them. Let's take a look at each of these and what they might sound like.

The fear voice will often emerge as:

- Loud
- Urgent
- Panicky
- Constant
- Catastrophizing
- Intrusive
- Demanding

It can be critical and judgmental, and it's often hard to turn the fear voice down. Fear very often feels tense or constricting in the body. We might notice a rapid heart rate or shallow breathing with fear.

Then we have our inner narratives, those stories we explored in the previous chapter. This inner narrative is often molded by our caregivers' voices and beliefs, by society, and the expectations we absorbed growing up. While these voices can offer valuable lessons, they may also impose limiting beliefs that do not serve us, causing self-doubt or making us question our abilities and worth.

Our inner narrative might sound like:

- You can't do this.
- Who do you think you are?
- What will people think?
- You're not good enough.
- You're wasting your time.
- Everyone is judging you.
- You're going to fail.

Our inner narratives, fears, and critical voices can be real jerks, and they do love to hijack our minds. Very often these voices are rooted in our past wounds or worries about the future. The good news is, they are not our intuition. Our inner wisdom will never make us feel bad or put us down, so if the voice sounds like that, it's simply not your intuition.

Fear, inner narratives, and critical self-talk can all be barriers to our connection with our inner guidance. Intuition can be quite subtle, especially at first; it comes through gently. That's why self-awareness and discovery are important, as well as tuning in and learning how our own inner wisdom manifests. The more we can understand ourselves and this "voice," the clearer it becomes.

Our inner wisdom is just information. It's not a long-winded and detailed description or roadmap of what to do and why. It's simple and subtle.

This past holiday season, my husband and I were in constant gift-hiding mode from the kids, trying to keep the magic alive. And one afternoon, I was waiting to get my kids off the bus when I checked the mailbox and saw there was a package. I very clearly heard my inner guidance say, "Don't leave it." That's all it said, simple and clear. But then I began to rationalize with myself, *Well, if I take it, the kids will see it, and they'll ask what it is,* and I wanted to avoid all of that. So I overrode that inner voice and told myself I would leave it and come back and grab it later. But when I went back that evening, the package had been stolen right out of our mailbox.

Now, my inner wisdom had information I didn't, but it also didn't scare me and say, "Don't leave the package, or someone will steal it." It was simple, subtle, and focused on the present moment.

That's what I mean when I say our inner wisdom will not use fear, even when the circumstances might be scary or there is risk. If your inner voice is rattling off all the negative possibilities or "what ifs," that's the fear voice.

Now that we understand the difference between our intuitive voice and those other voices, the next step is to really tune in and begin strengthening the muscle of listening. There are many different exercises and practices to deepen our connection to intuition and begin fostering that trust. I have outlined here eight of the practices I recommend most and have used myself.

Practices for Hearing Your Inner Wisdom

Developing a connection with ourselves and the ability to hear our inner voice requires stillness, consistency, and a willingness to trust. With time, practice, and patience, you will develop an unwavering trust in your inner voice and in yourself.

Meditation for Inner Listening

Meditation has so many benefits, including stress reduction, enhancing cognitive function, and improving our overall well-being. It can also be a beautiful tool for deeper connection with ourselves and our inner wisdom.

I like the way mindfulness-based stress reduction (MBSR) practitioners view meditation, which is as a tool allowing for greater self-exploration and awareness focusing on the present moment, the sensations of the body, and the awareness of thoughts and feelings. All of these are so important when developing a stronger connection with ourselves.

Meditation can feel difficult at first, but it is one of the best ways to develop your intuition. There are many different types of meditation: traditional sitting meditation, walking meditation, transcendental meditation. Finding the practice that resonates with you and feels safe in your body will be key—we're not trying to shock our system; we're trying to gently build a connection.

If you want to begin a sitting meditation and you've never done it before or you struggle to sit still, start small. Set a timer for one or two minutes and see how far you make it. Don't beat yourself up if you only make it 30 seconds; congratulate yourself and try again tomorrow. It's a practice, a muscle that you can build, just like any other muscle, so keep coming back.

One technique I find really helpful, and still use myself on especially fidgety days, is counting backward from 100. You can also pair your counting with your breathing, or simply focus on the in and out of the breath. Commit to doing this for 21 days without judgment or expectation, just allowing yourself to be present with the practice.

You might prefer to try guided meditation to start. I offer free guided meditations on my website. I also recommend the Insight Timer app, which hosts hundreds of meditations varying in length, so you're bound to find one that works for you.

The purpose of meditation is not to create a blank mind, but to be with whatever is there, taking an almost outside-looking-in approach with curiosity. It's totally normal for your mind to wander, and some days it will wander more than others. Patience and practice are key, but with a consistent meditation routine, you will reap so many benefits. As it becomes your daily practice, you will find that you can more easily access your intuitive voice and spiritual guidance within.

Journaling for Clarity

A journaling practice can offer deep self-reflection and profound insights. The pages of your journal can offer a safe container to explore feelings, patterns, thoughts, or anything that is on your mind. The practice of writing by hand is proven to create more presence and connection, slowing down our thoughts and bringing more of the subconscious mind to the surface.

Journaling is my go-to. When I started down this path almost 20 years ago, I began keeping a journal. I would write out my feelings, my goals, my fears, just pouring everything out and onto the pages. Sometimes, just the act of getting our thoughts out of our head creates more space between them, which leads to greater clarity.

Simple Ways to Use Your Journal for Intuitive Connection

- Each morning, preferably just upon waking or after your meditation practice, call in your spirit team and angels, and invite their guidance into your day. You can ask a simple question like "What do I need to know today?" or choose from any of the prompts on page 202. Then log what immediately comes to the forefront of your mind.
- Make it a point to log all the otherworldly occurrences that remind you that magic exists in the everyday: a feather you found, an intuitive nudge*, a vision you had—write it all!
- *An *intuitive nudge* is a subtle thought, feeling, or inner knowing. It might be about trying something new, or about a decision you have to make, but it doesn't come from a logical place, and it will continue to nudge us.
- After you record your intuitive nudges, come back and record when they are validated. If you acted on the nudge and it led to a beautiful outcome—write that down. This will help strengthen your trust in your intuition and deepen your connection to the universe.
- Write daily affirmations, or the new stories you created in the last chapter, to begin transforming your mindset and empowering your self-love journey.

- Continue to explore and release outdated ways of thinking that no longer serve you, allowing you to release limiting beliefs and embrace new ways of thinking.
- Try a meditation to connect with your inner wisdom before journaling. In my free Anchored meditation, I offer a guided meditation to tap into your heart's knowing. Record what comes up.

Journaling prompts to get you started:

- "What do I most need to know today?"
- "What is my heart asking me to do?"
- "What feels true for me today?"
- Think about a time when something happened, and afterward, you said, "I knew that was going to happen." How did you know?

By journaling, you can begin to create a dialogue with your inner self. It's a practice that, if you stick with it, will reveal so many insights and benefits that, over time, will transform your relationship with yourself.

Automatic Writing

Most of what trips up our access to our inner wisdom is our critical, logical, conscious mind stepping in to tell us all sorts of rational things like "That doesn't make any sense" or "That's just a coincidence" or "You sound really silly." To access our inner wisdom, or the universal intelligence within, we often have to go around that part of the brain. That's where automatic writing can help.

Automatic Writing is the act of writing without using the conscious mind. Neuroscience tells us that the process of writing in this way allows us to engage our right brain, the creative and intuitive side, while quieting our more logical left brain. Writing in this way is believed to come from the spiritual or the subconscious. It is *not* the same as keeping a journal. When we journal, we sort of word-vomit our thoughts, stresses, or questions onto the paper, working through it in logical or analytical ways, and we tend to write in the first-person "I."

Automatic writing comes from a different place; it's closer to a channeling experience. Call it spirit, the universe, your guides, angels, or simply your inner wisdom, but you can feel the difference in the guidance. When I began the process of channeling, I started with automatic writing.

I actually began this practice because I had been hearing soft, angelic music playing around me at various points throughout the day for weeks. At first, I was checking my phone, my husband's phone, and the TV to try to find the source of the music. I kept asking, "Does anyone hear that?" but no one else seemed to hear anything. Seeing and hearing things that others don't was my normal by this point, but I wasn't really sure what to do with this music. My mentor at the time suggested I try automatic writing whenever I heard the music, thinking of it as a sort of doorbell from spirit. So I did.

And I felt *really* silly at first, like I was talking to myself, or maybe I was making it all up. But I began getting bits of information that were undeniably from a higher source of wisdom. In fact, before I knew I was pregnant with my third daughter, I had an automatic writing session with my angel team, who told me I was pregnant, and it was a girl. Within a few weeks, I would find out that they were right.

How to Get Started with Your Own Automatic Writing

Choose a time where you will not be disturbed. This might be first thing in the morning or after your meditation practice. Start by setting your intention. This could be as simple as "I am open to receiving guidance from my higher self today." Then you can start writing what is coming through. It might sound like just your thoughts at first, but keep going, trying not to pick up your pen or pause. If it feels easier, you might also start by asking a question. It could be as simple as "What do I need to know today?" and begin writing. It's very important not to censor yourself.

Believing is key here. Trust that what is coming through is the message you are meant to be receiving. Remember that your intuitive information, and even guidance from spirit, will come through gently. It will not be loud or pushy, and it definitely will not be critical or full of anger or fear. If the messages coming through sound like this, it's not your higher wisdom; it's just your prerecorded mind.

You can do this at any time, but I find the best time is in the quiet and stillness of the morning, even before you've had a cup of coffee (eek! I know). But, in the fog of the early morning, you're still in between two worlds, and your overanalyzing mind hasn't quite kicked into drive yet. Even better, create a ritual out of it. Keep a journal next to your bed, and each morning, in the stillness, set an intention to hear and be open to receiving the messages for your highest good.

Automatic writing can be an excellent tool for channeling guidance from our higher selves. However, it's not a practice for everyone. Individuals with mental health concerns should consider consulting a healthcare professional before engaging in automatic writing. Approach your practice with care and trust yourself if you feel uncomfortable—it's not for you, and that's okay. There are so many practices to help develop and strengthen your intuition. Another one I recommend is rooted in play: pretending.

Let Yourself Pretend

Now, if you are struggling with the journaling or automatic writing, I want you to try this different approach.

Pretend.

Yes, I did just say pretend, and here's why: When we want to strengthen our intuitive practice, we can get so caught up in rigidity and putting pressure on ourselves, worrying if we're doing it right, that we end up blocking our own connection. Pretending takes the pressure off and gives us space to play and allow imagination and curiosity to take over. Research shows that pretending allows us to engage our imagination, which operates in our subconscious. When we can engage from this place, it actually allows us to access intuitive insights and subconscious information more freely. This is the same reason you have all your "Aha!" moments in the shower or while driving, because there is zero pressure to be doing anything or performing, and you're more relaxed.

I know you haven't played pretend in decades. But hear me out. What's the only rule of pretend? There are literally no rules. And if there are no rules, you can't make a mistake. And if you can't make a mistake, maybe your judgmental and critical voice will quiet down and allow you to just receive the guidance that is already within you.

Pretend is a technique I have used in my intuitive art workshops when folks are apprehensive about putting paintbrush to canvas, feeling like they don't know where to start. It might feel silly at first, but allow yourself to try. Everyone has the ability to tap into their intuition. Don't put so much pressure on yourself. Make some space to loosen and play and have fun.

Try this: Grab a journal and pen and set a timer for 10 minutes. You can pretend any scenario, but perhaps try pretending you are a wise oracle with access to a realm of inner wisdom (it's okay if you think it's silly; we're just pretending). You can even dress the part! I'll get vulnerable here and tell you that I have a hand-sewn, black-and-emerald-green hooded cape that I made for myself. It came to me in a vision and was a fun creative project. Sometimes, I put it on when I meditate because it helps me feel into my own power: dressing the part and immersing in the role. So, there you go. I play dress-up with a hand-sewn cape; you can pretend to be a wise sage for 10 minutes.

Now, ask yourself an open-ended question. Just for those 10 minutes, allow yourself to write from your intuitive voice (that wise oracle within), and if you feel silly, or you're not sure it's your intuition, let yourself pretend it is anyway—no one is going to read this! Leave judgment at the door, and let imagination take over, giving yourself space to believe that what is coming through is in fact your intuition. See what happens. How does it feel? What comes up?

If you keep your journal with all your "pretend" intuitive wisdom, you will begin to notice that it's actually really smart, sage advice you're giving yourself. Come back to the journal and record when that advice was spot on, and gradually, you will be shifting out of pretend and into direct access with your inner wisdom.

I promise.

Another practice is one we touched on earlier in the book: body awareness. Becoming aware of your body as a partner in intuition.

Body Awareness

If you ask any psychic or medium, they will tell you that they use their senses to pick up on information. And if you think about the Clair senses, they are simply our physical senses heightened. I truly believe one of the most important first steps in strengthening our intuitive muscle is to develop a partnership with our bodies. That's why I dedicated an entire section of the book to coming back into partnership with your body. We can strengthen our connection to our senses with a little practice. First, let's look at what the different Clairs are.

Clairvoyance, or Clear Seeing, is the psychic ability of picking up subtle information through enhanced vision or your mind's eye. People who are Clairvoyant often see visions or mental images, have vivid dreams, or can even see auras. They might also see spiritual beings, angels, guides, or loved ones in spirit.

Clairaudience, or Clear Hearing, is the psychic ability of picking up subtle information through sounds. People who are Clairaudient might hear ringing in their ears, or hear voices of spirit, angels, or loved ones in spirit. These voices or sounds can be disembodied, meaning external, or heard within. They might hear music, bells, conversations, or other sounds that others cannot hear.

Clairsentience, or Clear Feeling, is the psychic ability of picking up information through your sense of feelings or physical sensations within the physical body. People who are clairsentient might get goose bumps when something is true or feel a tension in their stomach if something is off. They might experience headaches if someone close to them has a headache or feel chills with the heavy energy of a space.

Clairempathy, or Clear Emotions, is the psychic ability of picking up information through clear emotional feeling.

Empaths are clairempathic in that they can feel someone else's emotions as if they are their own. Clairempaths do not need to be within proximity of a person to feel their emotions, as they can pick them up across time and space.

Claircognizance, or Clear knowing, is the psychic ability of knowing information without any logical reason or access to that information. Claircognizants might know who is calling before the phone rings or be able to tell when someone is lying. They might be able to predict events or make big decisions with ease from this place of knowing.

We all have psychic abilities. Some might manifest more easily than others, but with practice, we can access and strengthen these abilities. Let's try a simple exercise to get started.

Simple Exercise

Take a moment to connect with your body, either by becoming aware of your breath or noticing the weight of your arms in your lap. Just bring your awareness to your body. Next, think about a decision you're facing: This could be whether to send the kids to that summer camp or as simple as if you should order pizza for dinner.

Choose an answer, yes or no, and then notice how your body reacts. Does the answer feel expansive or contracted? An expansive feeling might feel light, airy, and indicate a yes, whereas a constricted feeling might be tense, or restricting, and indicate a no. You will have to practice to learn how your own body responds and how the information shows up for you, because we are all different. Try this throughout your day with little decisions you have to make and remember to record your body's responses in your journal.

By incorporating the mindfulness practices we've discussed, as well as the body scan from Chapter 7, you will begin to deepen your connection with these Clair abilities and the inner wisdom in your body.

Oracle Cards

Oracle cards are a divination tool used for spiritual and intuitive guidance. Some intuitives find divination tools like tarot or oracle cards helpful when developing their trust in their inner wisdom. Others prefer to develop their intuition and then bring in the tools. Personally, I prefer to journal and get clear on my own inner voice before bringing in any cards. But there is no right or wrong way, as everyone is different and everyone learns differently, so feel into what is right for you.

Oracle cards differ from tarot in that there is no set system or structure that you follow. I prefer oracle for this reason! Tarot has 78 cards divided into the Major and Minor Arcana with specific archetypes and meanings. Whereas oracle cards differ widely in their themes, imagery, and structure, which allows for more flexibility and intuitive reflection. The symbolism and open-ended nature of oracle cards allow us to tune in to our own inner guidance and reflect on what it means to us, interpreting from a place within, which is why these can be great practice for building trust in your own inner voice and your ability to interpret its messages.

Techniques for using oracle cards:

- As with all of these practices, start with a sacred space.
- If this is a brand-new oracle deck, consider a connection practice such as meditating with the cards and cleansing them with your favorite smoke cleansing or visualization practice. Some folks like to reflect on each card to get familiar with it and understand its energy.

- Once you have a connection with your deck, tune in and connect with your heart center; this can be done by sitting in stillness or taking a few centering breaths.
- Shuffle your cards and spread them face down on the table in front of you.
- Set your intention. What are you looking for guidance on? I recommend asking open-ended questions like "Thank you for guiding me to understand my next move at work" rather than "Will I get a promotion soon?"
- If you are brand new to this, just pull a single card to avoid confusion or overwhelm.
- Draw the card and use your own inner guidance to interpret its meaning. If your oracle deck comes with an interpretation for each card, try to interpret it yourself before consulting the author's interpretation. This will help you build your intuitive muscle, and you will probably be validated upon reading the author's interpretation.
- If it helps, write down the question you asked, the card you pulled, and your own interpretation of it. Include in your notes any visions, feelings, knowings, sounds, or other messages that came through and how you received them. Practice and log it.

As with any of these practices, doubt will probably creep in, leaving you unsure of your interpretation or ability. When this happens, try connecting with your breath and reminding yourself that you are highly intuitive and there is no wrong way to do this. Experiment with what works for you and stay open and curious while leaving judgment aside.

Dream Journaling

We've all had dreams of losing our teeth or showing up to work naked, only to wake up the next morning wondering, *What was that about?* after a night of intense dreaming. Dreams can tell us so much about ourselves and our lives. They can show us parts of ourselves and our emotional states. They can be rich with symbolism. Or they can be visitation dreams, in which our loved ones pop in to say hello. Your spirit team and higher wisdom use dreams to communicate with you. For the purpose of strengthening your intuition, I think it's important to look at all the layers of dreams.

I'll share a personal story with a recurring dream. For years, I had a recurring dream about being bitten by a snake. The scenario would always be different: in my house, in the yard, finding it on me, reaching under something, and it would latch on. The circumstances changed, but the theme was the same: In a panic, I would grab the snake by its head to try and prevent it from biting me, and I would always get bitten.

I had this recurring dream at least once a month for over a decade. When I was working with my naturopath to help with some of my medical issues, we decided to try a homeopathic remedy. The instructions were: I was to take the remedy, and over the following three days, just take notice of what comes up. Well, for the following three nights, I dreamt about the snake.

The first night, I grabbed the snake by the head, only I didn't get bitten. The second night, the snake was on my back, where I couldn't grab it, and I didn't get bitten. The third night, the snake was on the floor looking up at me; we stared at each other, and then it slithered away in the opposite direction. I knew there was so much healing taking place in these dreams, just on the sheer fact alone that I was no longer being bitten by this snake. Snakes often represent transformation or fear. But intuitively for me, the snake represented my own inner turmoil and tendency to be highly self-critical, attack myself, and suppress my anger. As I healed the relationship with myself, my relationship with the snake in my dreams was also changing in that it wasn't attacking me, and it didn't have so much control over me.

Dreams can be rich with symbolism, and I'll share some of the more common dream symbolism in this section, but I encourage you to always reflect on your intuitive understanding of your dreams before consulting any mainstream symbolism.

If you have a recurring dream yourself, that can be a great place to start, because there is likely a hidden message within that is wanting to be known. Reflect on whether you have a recurring dream and what it could possibly mean in your own life. Journal about it, and tap into your intuitive interpretation of the message.

Techniques for dream recall:

- Set an intention before going to sleep. This could sound like "I want to have a dream that will show me how to finish this project" or "I want to have a dream that will help me understand my next steps in my business." Call in your angels and spirit team and thank them for helping you to see the answers, or roadblocks, whatever you are looking for.

- Keep a journal next to your bed, and as soon as you wake up in the morning, quickly jot down what you remember from your dreams. Our waking state, before we have gotten up to use the bathroom or have coffee, is a sort of in-between-two-worlds state. If journaling isn't for you, you can try voice recording what you remember.
- Recall how you felt emotionally in the dream. Was it tense and stressful, or did you feel happy and at peace? Our emotional states can tell us a lot.
- When trying to interpret symbols, I always recommend using your own inner knowing to interpret versus asking the Internet what an image or symbol might mean. Symbols can vary in meaning across cultures and people; you will always have a personal feeling about a symbol that will be stronger than a widely used interpretation.
- Like any of these practices, consistency is key. Make a commitment to stick with it, and you will begin to notice recurring themes or symbols, which will better help you understand the messages within your dreams.

Here are some common dream symbols and what they could mean, but as always, please reflect on your own intuitive understanding of your dreams first:

Death	Transformation, new beginnings
Teeth Falling Out	Loss of control, anxiety
Flying	Expansion, freedom, new perspectives
Water	Emotions (depending on the state of the water, it can represent calm or turbulence)
Being Naked	Vulnerability, embarrassment, exposure, or visibility
Falling	Insecurity, instability, fear of failure
Being Chased	Conflict, fear, hiding from something
Animals	Animal symbolism can vary widely, but will often be linked to the qualities of that animal

Dreams can offer a treasure trove of messages and intuitive insights. With consistent practice logging your dreams, you will begin to notice themes arise and be able to strengthen your intuitive interpretation of what they mean to you. Don't be surprised if you start to receive answers and guidance from your spirit team through dream messages.

Creative Expression

The one thing I have witnessed in guiding others through the creative process is that when the voice is not there, either due to physical or emotional reasons, creativity is a mode of communication: both with others and with ourselves. It's a chance to be seen. A chance to tell our story. A chance to *know* our story. The creative process is so closely connected to the soul.

If you watch a child create, they do so very freely and without instruction. They aren't trying to win artist of the year or host a gallery viewing; they are staying present and allowing the energy to flow through them. Unfortunately, as we grow, we quickly learn to color in the lines. To create for others and for rewards. We look to our parents or teachers to guide us to what is right and what is true. And while this is not necessarily bad or wrong, we begin an outward search for our answers. We learn that we can't trust ourselves or that we can't trust our feelings. Then we say things like "I'm not intuitive" or "I'm not creative." When really, being intuitive and creative is part of being human—and often a big part of being highly sensitive.

Creative Expression Practice: Where do we begin when we have cut ourselves off from this connection and form of expression for so long? First things first, like all of these practices, let go of judging yourself or striving for perfect. You do not need to be a professional artist to create. It's about letting go of expectations and outcomes and simply trusting yourself. Give yourself time and space to connect with your heart, and allow the process to unfold. There are no mistakes here.

We've already discussed how pouring your energy into worrying about whether you are doing it right, or about how it looks, will only block your intuition. Trust yourself and create from the heart center, not the mind. Be present with the experience, allowing yourself to remain open to intuitive messages that might come through. It doesn't have to be all serious and hard work either. In fact, that's a good indicator that you are in your head. Experiment, play, and really loosen up: use your hands, make a mess, let go. Whether your creative process is writing, drawing, painting, sculpting, or even dancing, let yourself get to a place where you are flowing, using the process of creating as an extended mindfulness meditation. Here are some tips for getting started:

- Put on some music.
- Focus on the sensation of movement: the movement of muscles in the hands, the breath as it moves in and out of the lungs.
- Approach the creative process with intent, and practice mindfully and consciously. The idea here is to simply be present with yourself.
- As you are moving through the creative process, take note of what is coming up for you. Be aware of any thoughts or feelings. If you would like, write these down in a journal.
- If it helps, before you start, tell yourself this is not for anyone else to see. You don't have to hang it up, frame it, publish it, or show anyone—it's allowed to be messy.

Creative expression is an ability we all possess. It's a tool for self-discovery and a process that connects us deeply with our inner wisdom and our soul, strengthening our understanding of ourselves and unearthing the many layers that make us who we are.

We've discussed several practices to help tune in and connect with the inner voice. Pick one or two and give them a try. Find what works for you, and let it be okay that there will be moments of questioning yourself, and even some days where it feels like you're not connected at all. I still have days like that!

Key Takeaways

Learning to trust ourselves and our inner guidance is a gift worth working for. The more we can become aware of our internal dialogues and differentiate between what is fear or inherited narratives, and what is actual inner guidance, the easier it becomes to understand how our inner voice shows up for us.

Obstacles are normal and will happen no matter where you are in your journey! Like how I refused to listen to my inner voice and decided to leave the gift in the mailbox. We're all human, and we'll have moments where we overthink, or we're tired, or we search externally for some validation. Don't beat yourself up if you're having a hard time or feel like you should be further along. Putting pressure on yourself or being overly critical is a surefire way to shut down that inner voice. Like anything else, practice is key. Think of it like building a muscle. You wouldn't walk into the gym, lift a five-pound weight once, and expect to be a bodybuilder overnight. Consistency and patience are required. The more you use your inner wisdom and trust yourself, the easier it will become.

11

Finding Your Voice

How to Reclaim Your Power

When I first started my business social media account, it would take me days, weeks even, to post a single post. I would write and rewrite my content and then read and reread my words, searching for anything that might be picked apart or taken the wrong way. After I pressed Post, I would be overcome with fear. It was the same wave of fear that would crash into me every time I tried to share my opinions, needs, or my voice at all. As I have expressed throughout this book, sharing these parts of myself just didn't feel safe.

We have discussed many of the reasons we might mute our voices along the way, from childhood experiences to carrying the Witch Wound. Whatever it was, somewhere along the way, you may have lost yourself. Your big, beautiful heart could only hold so much until the pain caused you to hide and slowly disappear. But you didn't actually disappear; you are still there. If you take nothing else away from this book, I want you to begin to remember who you are.

There is a little version of you inside, a version who has endured so much, and she is waiting for you to remember your own strength and power. You know she is there, you can feel her, and you've been trying so hard to help her, searching everywhere for the answers. But she doesn't need answers; she just needs you to remember. She needs you to remember that you have always had the ability to choose, and the first step is reclaiming your inner authority.

In Part II of this book, we looked at many of the ways our modern world is designed to disconnect us from our own agency. The design is sensitive averse: loud, fast, urgent, and tough. Have you ever stopped to ask yourself why that might be? What if it's because we are actually incredibly powerful, and if we understood our own potential and divinity, and could access our sensitivity as an ability, not a flaw, those systems would lose their hold over us?

The reason why I don't believe there is a simple blueprint for this type of reclaiming ourselves is because following someone else's plan would diminish the reclamation. We've surrendered our power most of our lives: to authority figures, to our caregivers, to our relationships, to our jobs. We've silenced ourselves and shrunk ourselves, hiding pieces away for our own survival. Part of the healing is realizing that we've always held the keys to our own freedom. Sometimes I still find it hard to imagine or believe how much power we actually have. I think if we truly understood, it would blow our minds.

In order to remember this inner force, we have to first stop giving it away. Reclaiming our agency and connection isn't about following someone else's plan or searching for external answers; it's about cultivating trust in ourselves. And that's not to say that we must do it alone; there will be times on our journey that we need support from a teacher, a therapist, our community, friends, and family. But that support should always feel empowering and move us into deeper alignment and connection with ourselves; it should never leave us feeling unworthy, reliant on another person or group, or afraid.

The uncharted path home to ourselves can be both messy and beautiful, and it will be unique for each of us. You have the power to decide what your journey looks like, when to take each step, and how far you wish to go. That's the true beauty of this experience: It's yours to choose. The act of being true to yourself and learning to honor who you are will always be worthwhile.

I might not be able to give you the blueprint to follow, but hopefully, the areas we have explored already have been meaningful and have helped you think about your own experiences and needs. In the final chapter of this book, I will help you discover for yourself your own blueprint by bringing together all the practices and prompts we've discussed throughout and inviting you to personalize your own map forward. Let's get into the final piece of this book, where we will reclaim our voice and create a vision for ourselves.

Expression

Adverse childhood experiences can leave us feeling like we don't have a voice. We might feel unheard or unseen, unsafe, or unworthy of taking up space. The impact of our early experiences can be very complex and will differ widely between each of us.

We've discussed the reasons behind why we might tend to self-silence or abandon ourselves as highly sensitive women, such as to avoid conflict or seek approval, or because of societal expectations and conditioning, or because growing up, it was just our way to keep ourselves safe. And we discussed how detrimental this can be to our own well-being and even health. But the most difficult cost of our silence, in my opinion, is the complete erosion of self. We disconnect from our heart and soul, and over time, we may feel like we've forgotten who we are entirely. Or worse, maybe we never even had the chance to find out who we are. This chapter is all about remembering ourselves and making different choices.

Coming back to ourselves can feel like an identity crisis, like someone just turned the lights on in a house we've spent our lives living in but have never actually seen. At first, you might not even know what your favorite food or color is. Remember to move gently; it's a rediscovery, walking through those halls and witnessing what has been inside.

Reclaiming our voice and giving ourselves permission to be seen and heard is a crucial part of coming home to ourselves, and one of my favorite practices to strengthen our connection to our voice and build the muscle of expression is to chant.

Finding Your Voice Through Chanting

Chanting has so many benefits. And, if you just recoiled at even the thought of chanting, stick with me; I am not going to ask you to hold a tune or apply to be Taylor Swift's backup singer.

Sometimes, when my kids are all bickering and no one is listening, and it's been a long day, and I'm overwhelmed, feeling like I want to scream, I choose to sing instead. It calms me down immediately, it makes my kids laugh, and it allows me to express myself in a safe way for everyone.

Singing and chanting create vibrations in our body. Remember in Chapter 6 how we discussed the healing impact of vibrations and sound? Think about that impact from inside our own bodies. Let's take a look at some of the perks of chanting.

The benefits:

- It's a stress reducer.
- It encourages us to focus and be present with ourselves.
- It's an emotional release or expressive outlet.
- It releases endorphins.
- It helps with memory recall (we can all recite our favorite song from when we were kids even if we haven't heard it in decades).
- Chanting encourages the flow of energy through the throat, which creates a vibration that supports balance of the energy center there and promotes a clearer self-expression (hello, Witch Wound!).

As with every practice in this book, I wouldn't recommend it if it wasn't something I have already practiced myself. Chanting has become a staple of my own rituals. And for those who still feel self-conscious at just the idea, I get it. When I first started my chanting, I would hide myself away in the house, worried my own family or the UPS delivery person might hear me and judge me. But now, I can be heard down the block chanting, and my family is used to it. Before each of my private sessions with clients, I do at least 10 minutes of chanting to really connect with my voice and my power. Try it! You don't have to perform for anyone; just get into the practice of finding and connecting with your voice and see how it feels.

First, decide which one speaks to you more: chanting or singing? And have it in easy reach on your phone or computer. Here are some ideas to get you started:

- Chanting your favorite affirmations
- Singing your favorite song (be mindful of choosing one that doesn't disrupt your energy, i.e., make you feel sad or low)
- Making a simple sound, just to get comfortable with the vibration in your body, like Om (Aum), which is a sacred syllable deeply rooted in Indian spiritual traditions and is widely used as a chant during meditation
- Listening to Kyle Gray's album *Radiant Aura*, which is a beautiful blend of mantras, spiritual chants, and ambient soundscapes that you can pick and choose from. One of my favorites.
- Using online resources like YouTube, where you can find guided meditations and chanting for beginners
- Using apps like Insight Timer, which has guided chanting and mantras available

Experiment with a few and see how they feel. Always listen to yourself.

Then, make it a practice:

- Find a quiet and safe space where you feel comfortable and will not be afraid of being judged.
- You might try connecting with your breath first by taking a few nourishing breaths in.
- Choose an intention to connect with during your practice; this could be "I am allowed to be heard," "My voice matters," or "I am powerful."
- Then perhaps start by humming. You can hum your favorite song or just a simple tune that you know, like "Happy Birthday" or a famous nursery rhyme.
- Feel the hum as it vibrates in your body.
- Notice if any emotions or feelings arise.
- Afterward, you can journal anything that might have come up for you.

Commit to practicing for just a few minutes every day, and see how things might shift for you. You might start to notice a growing connection to your voice, or find you are speaking up in meetings or sharing an opinion with more ease and confidence. Your voice might have been the thing that was silenced, but as you strengthen your connection to it, you will begin to remember how crucial it is for communicating not only your wants, needs, and boundaries, but for the expression of who you are in this lifetime.

Let's explore how our connection to our voice translates into the very important practice of boundaries.

Boundaries

Remember how I shared that, years ago, sleep-deprived and afraid, I walked into the office of a renowned spiritual healer for help? Clutching a pillow, sinking into her couch, I reluctantly informed her that, for the better part of almost six years, I had been experiencing nocturnal visitors in the form of inaudible voices, swirling lights, and figures standing at the end of my bed. Then I paused and waited for her to tell me I was crazy.

Instead, it was in this first session that I learned I was in charge of my energetic space, and I learned how to set boundaries with spirit to keep my peace. I often joke that I learned how to set boundaries with the dead before I ever learned how to set boundaries with the living.

As I shared throughout the book, it was my own body that eventually taught me about boundaries with the living. When I finally began to tune in to the physical aspect, I realized how my body constricted around certain people. Or how, when I swallowed my words to keep the peace, I felt that tension pooling in my stomach. My body would tighten when I performed and played nice instead of speaking up for myself. It was continuously showing me where I was moving out of alignment or abandoning myself. As highly sensitive people, our bodies will often reject people, places, and even foods that are not in alignment with us. It's all part of the magic within.

But boundaries can feel like a foreign language when we have spent our whole lives overriding our own needs. If we were never modeled healthy boundaries or weren't allowed to express our needs, it can feel really challenging. But it is a skill that can be learned, and like anything else, it gets easier with practice. Before we can even begin to communicate our boundaries, though, we have to be in connection with ourselves and understand what we actually want and need.

Understanding Our Needs

What do we need? As highly sensitive folks, the lines can be blurry between our own emotions and needs, and those of others. This confusion often arises from prioritizing others' needs, causing us to completely lose touch with our own. Developing self-awareness and trust helps us tune in to and understand our own needs more clearly.

Practicing Awareness and Self-Trust

Here are steps to help you tune in with your body and begin listening to its guidance:

- **Awareness**: Notice how your body and energy respond to your world throughout the day. What makes you feel tense and restricted? What makes you feel safe and expansive?
- **Curiosity**: What is your body trying to tell you? What is the need?
- **Name It**: You don't have to express it to anyone yet; just name it for yourself and practice doing so.
- **Trust Yourself**: You know what you feel, even if this is your first time naming it. Trust yourself.

Why Do We Need Boundaries?

Setting boundaries can be a form of self-love and self-care. They allow us to share our needs with others, showing how we would like to be treated and respected.

For us highly sensitive folks, boundaries around our time and space can help avoid overwhelm and can help us maintain our identity so we don't get swept up in other people's stuff. Healthy boundaries allow us to have authentic and respectful relationships and a better balance of prioritizing ourselves and our needs.

How to Set Boundaries

You can read entire books dedicated to the art of setting boundaries or spend years in therapy role playing how to share your needs with others. I think we can make boundaries feel like this big, difficult thing. But it's actually very simple. Not easy, but simple. It's about communicating and expressing who we are and what we need to other humans. That can feel almost impossible when we've shut that part of ourselves down. But it's a piece that we have been working to heal, slowly, throughout this book.

I don't recommend setting your first-ever boundary with anyone in your life who doesn't feel like a safe person. Start with your safest friend or partner, the person who knows you best and is open to receiving all of who you are. Start small: Maybe you don't want to go to the party that is scheduled this weekend because you really need to prioritize rest and recharge your social battery after a busy week. Remember that you are allowed to have needs, like resting and recharging; you are allowed to have wants, like wanting to stay home;

and you are allowed to share those with the people who want to be in relationship with you.

As you begin using your voice and speaking up for yourself, pay attention to any physical sensations that might arise and allow them to be signals. Maybe it feels really scary, and you notice an unease in your stomach; allow that sensation to be with you; welcome it in. Maybe you feel really drained after sharing your needs for the first time. That's okay, let yourself rest after and take care of yourself for having the courage and strength to choose yourself. For people that have always had space to set healthy boundaries, this might sound silly, but for people like you and me who are figuring this out for ourselves and for the first time, it is going to feel big, and that's okay. Honor your own experience and seek out the people who will honor you through it.

You are allowed to protect your peace. You are allowed to limit time with energy vampires and carve out time to recharge and say no to what drains you.

You are allowed.

We know the importance of having healthy boundaries to maintain our well-being and protect our relationships, but setting them can prove to be challenging, especially for us highly sensitive folks.

Challenges Highly Sensitive Folks Might Face

- Having a hard time saying no, especially as we empathize with others' situations
- Fear of losing the relationship or upsetting others
- Difficulty understanding what we want or need, or differentiating between our wants and needs and those of others

- Fear of how others will respond
- Folding in on ourselves if conflict arises

Remember, self-compassion is key when you are learning a new skill. It will probably feel pretty difficult at first. We all have our limits, and it's okay to prioritize your well-being without feeling guilty.

One thing I always feel is important to mention when discussing boundaries is that not everyone is safe to set boundaries with. When I discuss boundaries and having limits, I am referring to your safe people. The friends and family who love you and want to be in a balanced and respectful relationship with you. If you are in an unsafe relationship, physically or emotionally, or in an unsafe environment, this is not the place to begin setting boundaries. Your safety will always be paramount; please seek out professional help first.

You deserve to feel safe and to have safe people in your life who make you feel seen, heard, loved, and respected.

As you continue on your journey of self-expression and setting boundaries, be gentle with yourself and celebrate the small wins. I promise, like any other practice in this book, it is a muscle that we build, and over time, it gets easier and easier.

Committing to Yourself

Nothing will deteriorate your trust in yourself faster than making commitments to yourself and breaking them. Even if this is how you have operated your whole life, you can start committing to yourself now by committing to small, meaningful actions that align with you and your values.

In this section I want to encourage you to deeply reflect on what truly matters to you and what kind of life you not only want to lead but know is possible for you. Remember your power here. One of the key themes that spirit has shown me on my journey back to myself has been about highly sensitive souls, the ones who have felt powerless, who have given so much of themselves in service of others, and how this is the time to start to turn that energy back into themselves. When we can do this, the ripple effect out into the world will be enormous. It's almost like we've been going about it the wrong way. It's not about giving all of ourselves; it's about giving to ourselves first so we are energized, and in our peace and power, we'll be able to change the world around us. Keep this in mind as you embark on the rest of this chapter.

Define Your Core Values

As you remember who you are and decide how you want to write your own story, start by reflecting on your personal core values. These are the principles that are most important to you. Try to come up with three or four things that are aligned with what is important to you. What do you stand for? What do you believe in? These will become your guiding principles as you move forward on your journey. These may change over time, so don't get stuck here.

Examples of core values:

- Integrity
- Humor
- Loyalty
- Honesty
- Respect
- Authenticity
- Empowerment
- Beauty
- Peace
- Curiosity

If you are looking at this list feeling overwhelmed and not sure where to start, consider these questions to get the juices flowing:

- What qualities do you admire most in others?
- What do you want to be remembered for?
- What sort of impact do you want to have?
- What upsets you most? What values are being challenged in these situations?

Looking at these lists, and after a bit of quiet reflection, grab your journal and jot down a few core values that you feel called to. My personal core values that I live by and run my business by are honesty, integrity, and humor. The above is not a comprehensive list, so explore for yourself what is important to you and keep them at the forefront as you continue forward.

Create Your Vision

Your personal vision for yourself and your life is incredibly powerful. If you have felt like your life has been on autopilot up until this point, now is your chance to press the Pause button and decide what you actually want for yourself. What do you want your life to look like? Really spend some time on this section and get clear. Think about how you want to feel. And if that feels too hard, start with how you don't want to feel anymore and work from there.

Look back at the values you listed and what life would look like to live by those values. If one of the values you chose for yourself is peace, but you are currently living in what feels like chaos, imagine what peace would look like in your life.

How would it feel? What would your day-to-day activities be in a life centered around peace? Don't freak out if those daily activities feel like an enormous leap from your daily life right now. We're just in the imagining phase; action comes later. Spend a bit of time on this vision, because we will be using it again at the end of the chapter.

Example: If your vision for yourself is centered around your core values of authenticity and peace, your vision might look something like:

- Living in a peaceful home that is filled with love and respect
- Working for yourself and setting your own schedule
- Spending quality time with family and close friends each week
- Not feeling rushed or overwhelmed in daily activities
- Having a ritual practice of daily meditation, yoga, or journaling
- Being safe to share your whole self, opinions, and ideas

What Is Your Guiding Statement?

Now that you've got your personal core values and vision, come up with your personal guiding statement. Your guiding statement should emphasize your values and vision. What message do you want to be your guide, the message you will reinforce every day? This is like your own affirmation, or mantra. As you make decisions for your life, you can come back to this guiding statement to make sure your decisions are aligned with the life you are trying to lead.

Example: Again, if your core values and vision centered around peace and authenticity, your guiding statement might sound something like:

"I am free to be myself and live my life authentically. I create deep inner peace and invite in more simplicity and loving relationships. I commit to aligning my actions with my values and inner wisdom, prioritizing myself, and leading a life I truly love."

Fill Out Your Soul Aligned Vision Below:

Core Values:

____

____

Personal Vision:

____

____

Personal Guiding Statement:

____

____

What's holding you back from this vision for yourself?
(i.e. fear, self-doubt, perfectionism, etc.)

____

____

What are some of the limiting beliefs you have been carrying?

____

____

Now that we are anchored in our values and vision, we are going to do an exercise of dreaming from this place of self-honoring, continuing from this heart-centered space of expanded energy and possibility.

Your Dream Wish List

In 2017, in our hotel room, shortly after we landed in Hong Kong, I got out a sheet of paper and began listing out what started as a bucket list: things I wanted to achieve before I died. I didn't date them or put them in any kind of order. I simply let myself dream about what I truly wanted in this life. That was only nine years ago, but I have already accomplished so many things on that list, including writing a book.

We are going to do a similar practice here by writing down your goals and dreams. The process of writing them down helps bring clarity and even a sense of priority and direction. Let yourself listen to your heart as you stay in the energy of wonder and exploration. Dream beyond the confines of what seems logical or practical. Don't focus on whether you can afford it, if it aligns with your life's purpose, or if you have enough time. Instead, dream from a place of possibility and openness.

Start by dividing your paper into five sections:

1. Relationships
2. Health and Wellness

3. Career and Purpose
4. Financial
5. Joyful Moments

Think about places you'd like to live or travel to. Reflect on experiences you've always wanted to pursue and your personal goals or dreams. Write them all down here without worrying about the how or when. Just allow yourself to dream freely!

For an even deeper practice, as you explore each section, include detailed descriptions. List the feelings you want to experience, and describe what those feelings look and sound like. The more specific you are, the clearer your vision for yourself will become!

Once you've completed this exercise, we are going to create the vision and focus on using the power of gratitude and heart-centered emotions to call forward the life we know is possible for us while taking aligned actions to help bring it into existence.

Holding the Vision Through Visualization

Visualization is a powerful tool that involves creating clear and detailed images in our mind. These can be directed at achieving certain outcomes or goals and are said to have the power to influence our reality. We see athletes do this all the time. Have you ever watched the Olympics and noticed the athletes sitting with their eyes closed right before their event? Many are holding the vision of the goal they have spent their life working toward. Even celebrities like Oprah have used visualization to drive their goals into reality.

This is a powerful visualization technique that I use with clients and have used to envision and bring to life my own goals. Once you have your completed values, vision, guiding statement, and dreams, you will have some clarity on what you envision for yourself moving forward.

Practice:

- First, ground and center yourself. I like to do this through breath connection and meditation, which we discussed earlier in the book.
- Once you're feeling nice and grounded, bring into vision a happy memory, something that makes you feel good, happy, warm, etc. Maybe it was sitting on the beach on your honeymoon or when your child took their first steps. You want it to be a memory that really fills you with a feeling of love, appreciation, and gratitude.
- Once you have the memory, try to engage all your senses. Bringing to mind all the visual details, what did it look like? Recall the smells, and how it felt (like the warm sun on your skin or the salty air falling sticky in your hair). Can you hear the laughter of your child as they stumbled? Get as detailed as possible until it feels like you are in this beautiful moment again.
- Try to picture it in your mind's eye, as if you are watching a replay of it.
- Once you are experiencing this past moment of love, warmth, and gratitude, it's time to shift and begin to bring into your vision the goal or outcome you are wanting to bring to life. Create an image of this, and bring it into your mental vision.

- Again, engage all five senses and imagine exactly what it would look like, in detail. Imagine how you would feel when you've achieved this. What is the setting? Who is there with you? What are they saying? Get as detailed as possible.
- Imagine this whole vision and the people in it surrounded in a beautiful, warm, pink light of love. Use your mind's eye to infuse the situation with loving energy.

You don't have to spend an hour doing this, just a few minutes. Once you've completed this, thank the universe, your spirit team, your angel guides, for assisting you toward this vision for yourself and for the highest good of all involved. Then release it. The key is to be consistent; practice this daily as you embark on your desired vision.

Action Creates Clarity

While we are more powerful than we understand, and the energy of visualizing can be magic, we also have to take aligned action, or nothing is going to change. Have you ever heard the Parable of the Drowning Man? The story goes that a man was stranded on the roof of his house during a flood, and he was praying to God to rescue him. He fully believed that God would come and save him, so he sat there and waited. As the floodwaters rose around him, a rowboat came to offer him safety, but the man declined, stating that God was coming to save him. So, the rowboat left. Next, a motorboat came by and offered to take the man to safety, but he declined, insisting that God was coming to save him. Finally, a helicopter arrived, lowering a rope for the man to be rescued, but he still declined, believing that God would come and save him.

Despite all the attempts at rescuing the man, he eventually drowned waiting for God. When he got to heaven, he confronted God, saying that he prayed for help and believed God would save him—why didn't God come to his recue? To which God replied, "I sent you a rowboat, a motorboat, and a helicopter. What more were you waiting for?"

It's a tale meant to illustrate that we cannot passively sit by and just hope for change. Divine intervention is only truly possible when we are also listening and taking aligned action. It's like teamwork.

While we have created this beautiful vision for our lives and for what we want and believe is possible, we now have to also continue to take the aligned steps to truly watch the magic unfold. Show the universe that you are serious with what you want for yourself, and the universe will respond. If you would like additional support with these practices, check out my Soul Aligned workshop, where we move through this process together.

Key Takeaways

Remembering your power is about remembering who you truly are, what you stand for, what you want and deserve, and then showing up in this world as the embodiment of that person.

Using your voice can be powerful. Understanding who you are and what you deserve is powerful. Remember your own divine connection within, and draw from that powerful source to help you move forward on your journey. Practice connecting to your power through chanting or singing, building your muscle to allow you to set boundaries that honor you. Use your voice, your words, and your vision to call into existence the life you deserve to live. One of safety, possibility, love, and joy.

The last chapter in this book is an invitation to create your own ritual for coming home to and honoring yourself. Reflect on what areas need your attention most, and use the tools that are offered as a guide inward. There is no wrong way—you've got this!

✳ 12 ✳

The Framework

Deciding for Yourself the Path Forward

Nine years ago, having worked my last day in corporate NYC and packed up our life's possessions to be shipped to Hong Kong, I had cut all the ties to my perfectly planned, pre-motherhood life. We had one stop before we left: to watch our best friends get married.

As I was sitting in carefully placed lawn chairs, the groom read from his note cards, his words pulling at an unexpected piece of my heart.

"I love how you are always unapologetically yourself," he declared to his new bride.

Those words.

It was the second wedding that year that a groom had publicly observed and admired this quality in his partner. And it was the second time that I felt this twinge of envy, a twinge that I didn't realize at the time was asking me to notice.

It was a quality I admired in others. A quality I didn't understand at the time.

How do they do that?

How are they not riddled with anxiety at trying to do everything right and make sure everyone around them approves of who they are?

Sitting in those lawn chairs, I had wished that someone could say those words about me: that I was unapologetically myself.

Over the course of this book, I outlined my own journey of the decade that followed and how I dismantled everything I knew in order to do exactly that for myself. I found my way home to me, the real me. Your own journey undoubtedly looks different, but perhaps you have noticed similar elements throughout this book.

My biggest hope for you, the reader, is that this book will help you cultivate an unwavering trust in yourself, deepening your connection to both body and inner wisdom, while finally making space for and letting go of what has been keeping you stuck, so that you can move forward with a life that supports and honors exactly who you are no matter where you are on your journey.

The journey of self-discovery has many names. Whether you call it healing, awakening, growing, or finding yourself, one thing is true: It is not a linear path. It has ups, downs, and often loops back to areas that still need our attention. It's a path we continuously walk. And while I cannot give you the map that will lead you home to yourself, I can share what helped me and offer a framework for you to chart your own map.

Designing Your Own Map

Throughout the book, we have discussed many different practices and tools. These are the practices that have supported me most on my own journey and the ones I offer to my clients. But maybe you're wondering how, or even when, to use these.

First, I invite you to reflect on what you've noticed about yourself throughout this book. What areas spoke to you most?

From there, we will look at the path of coming home to ourselves, broken into stages, along with the four core wounds we discussed in Part II. As you read through, notice for yourself where you feel you need the most support. Each of the practices discussed in the book are outlined, with the page you can find them on, and what area of the journey they will be most supportive for. Using this outline, you can create your own supportive ritual.

As a quick recap, these were the overall themes we looked at in each chapter:

The Entryway: In what ways are you honoring or neglecting your true self, and how does this affect the alignment between who you are and how you live?

Breaking the Silence: How freely and honestly do you express your true feelings and needs, and what holds you back from speaking your truth?

The Invitation: How willing are you to face all parts of yourself, including your discomfort, and do you approach these parts with acceptance or resistance?

Permission Slips: What truly defines your sense of worth, and how do patterns like people pleasing, perfectionism, or the need for control influence how you value yourself?

The Sensitivity Wound: How aware are you of your own sensitivity and empathy, and in what ways do you honor or manage its impact on your daily life and interactions with others?

The Connection Wound: How are fear and chronic stress affecting your ability to connect with your mind, body, and spirit?

The Body Wound: How connected are you to the wisdom and sensations of your body, and in what ways might past experiences or challenges be showing up physically or blocking you today?

The Witch Wound: How fully do you embrace your own divinity and spiritual abilities, and what fears or doubts might be holding you back from expressing and sharing them?

An Inside Job: What recurring patterns or limiting beliefs might be keeping you stuck, and what can you learn from the parts of yourself you tend to avoid?

An Ancient Wisdom: How much do you trust your own inner wisdom, and what keeps you from tuning in to it—whether it's self-doubt, inherited beliefs, or discomfort with stillness?

Finding Your Voice: How comfortable are you with identifying and expressing your own needs and boundaries, and what fears or uncertainties arise when you try to do so?

What have you learned about yourself?

____

____

____

____

____

Looking at themes, which area do you feel called to focus on most?

____

____

____

____

____

What areas do you feel the most resistance toward? Why might that be?

____

____

____

____

____

Let's take a look at the journey we just went on outlined in very clear stages. Using the following charts, and your own self-reflection, where do you feel you are in your own personal journey? Keep in mind that stages can overlap, the path is not linear, and the journey is continuous. Trust your intuition as you consider which stage best describes where you are right now.

Moving Toward Soul Alignment

In the visual below, you will find the stages of awakening or self-discovery. They are outlined in a circle that runs clockwise, although you might not find the path as clear and smooth, and that's okay. Under that you will see the four core wounds that you might experience, keeping in mind the wounds can correspond with any stage you are in.

The Path of Awakening

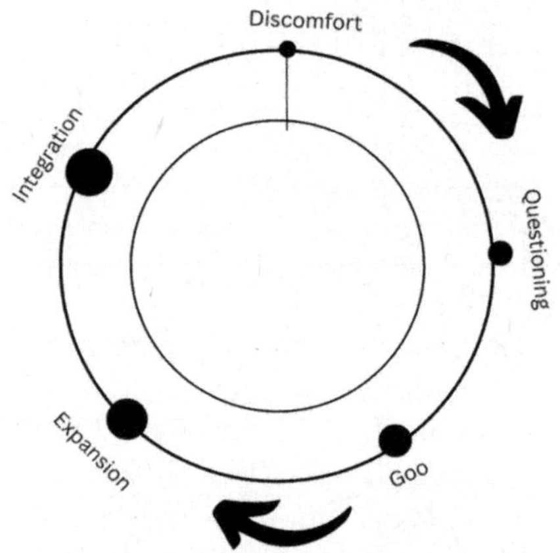

The Four Core Wounds

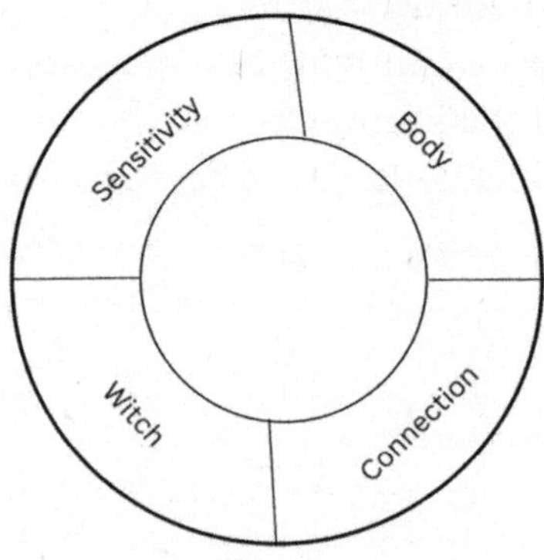

The Different Stages

Discomfort	Questioning	Goo	Expansion	Integration
Sense of unease, misalignment, feeling restless, and like something is just off	Intense self-reflection, questioning beliefs, values, ways of doing things, systems, and everything you previously accepted as truth	Profound transformation, shedding old ways and identities, facing your shadows	A sense of opening spiritually, heightened intuition, synchronicities, and a deeper connection to inner wisdom, a desire for learning	Embodying and applying what you've learned, greater flow, self-compassion, feeling like your true self and in greater alignment
Restlessness, unease, confusion, fatigue, frustration, "in a funk"	Confusion, loneliness, sadness, anger, overwhelm, vulnerability, uncertainty	Isolation, grief, loss, fear, disorientation, emotional intensity, hope	Curiosity, excitement, heightened sensitivity, clarity, wonder, empowerment	Peace, self-acceptance, confidence, ease, gratitude, alignment, fulfillment

The Four Core Wounds

Looking at the questions listed under each of the four core wounds in the following chart, which one feels like the one that might be impacting you most?

Hint: It might be the one you feel the most resistance to.

Sensitivity	Disconnection	Body	Witch
• Are you easily drained or overwhelmed? • Have you felt like your sensitivity is a flaw? • Do you resonate with being an empath or HSP? • Do you need alone time to recharge? • Do you feel like you pick up on other people's energies? • Has your sensitivity made you feel misunderstood? • Are you often prioritizing others over yourself?	• Do you feel like fear is running your life? • Does it feel like your nervous system is set on survival mode? • Do you struggle to rest or feel like rest must be earned? • Do you feel addicted to stress? • When you have down time, do you fill it with TV, scrolling social media, alcohol use, or online shopping to distract yourself? • Do you struggle with connecting to your emotions like anger, grief, or even joy? • Does it feel like you live in your head?	• Do you struggle with recurring symptoms? • Do you feel disconnected from your body? • Is it hard for you to feel good or even neutral about your body? • Do you often dismiss your own pain? • Do you have a history of adverse childhood experiences? • Do you notice recurring tensions or body sensations, stress or unease in any one area of the body?	• Do you have a feeling you were a healer, oracle, midwife, etc. in another life? • Do you feel like you have to silence yourself? • Are you afraid to be seen or to stand in your power? • Are you afraid of your own spiritual or psychic abilities? • Do you feel like you have to hide your spiritual or psychic abilities? • Do you feel unworthy of having divine connection?

Write down here what phase you're in and which wound or wounds most speaks to you.

Phase/s:

Wound/s:

Here are each of the practices we went through over the course of the book. Next to each one, I have listed which phase and wound they would be most supportive in as a guide for you to get started.

Energy hygiene practices: Listed on page 92, they're important for all phases and wounds but especially:

Phase: Expansion and Integration

Wound: Sensitivity and Connection

Energy hygiene can be practiced at any stage for general energetic well-being, but it is especially vital during these later stages, as sensitivity and energetic awareness heighten, and integration becomes the focus. If your wounds are sensitivity and connection, these practices help you to honor your sensitive nature and foster a practice of creating that time and space for stillness.

Body Scan and Body Map: Listed on page 138, they can be used at any time, but they're especially helpful for:

Phase: Discomfort, Goo, and Integration

Wound: Body and Witch

Body scan meditation and the body map are especially supportive in the early stages to manage discomfort and reconnect with the body, during the deep transformation of the Goo stage to process and ground yourself, and in the integration stage to embody and maintain new levels of awareness. These practices are especially helpful for healing the connection with the body, but for the Witch Wound as well, as it brings more awareness to body and psychic senses/abilities. It can be revisited at any point when grounding, relaxation, or self-connection are needed.

The Witch Wound Practices: Listed on page 154, they're supportive for all stages but especially:

Phase: Discomfort, Questioning, Expansion

Wound: Witch, Sensitivity, Connection

The Witch Wound practices involve reclaiming personal power, healing ancestral wounds, using your voice and reconnecting to your own divinity and psychic abilities. These practices can be supportive across all stages, but especially during the discomfort and questioning stages, as they can bring clarity and encourage self-compassion. And in the expansion stage as you tap further into your intuitive abilities and connection to the earth and universal energy.

Connection Practices: Listed on page 116, they're supportive for all stages, but especially:

Phase: Questioning, Goo

Wound: Connection, Body, Sensitivity

Practices like intentional rest, rediscovering joy, and writing to your inner child are about creating a sense of safety and wholeness again. These practices can be deeply supportive during the unraveling stages like Questioning and Goo. Joy, rest, and inner child work call us back into our bodies and ask us to honor ourselves and our needs.

Shadow Work: Listed on page 183, it's important as an ongoing practice, but it's especially helpful during:

Phase: Questioning, Goo, and Integration

Wound: All Wounds

Shadow work can and should be revisited throughout the soul-aligned journey, but it is especially transformative during the questioning and deep transformation phases, and it is integrated and ongoing for lasting change. It can be a helpful tool for each of the wounds to develop a deeper awareness of where they stem from.

Meditation: Listed on page 95, it's supportive of all phases and wounds, but it's best to begin gently with this practice.

Phase: All Phases

Wound: All Wounds

Meditation is supportive and beneficial in every stage of spiritual awakening. It helps manage discomfort, fosters self-awareness, can be grounding during transformation, expands our spiritual awareness, and can anchor us during integration. The specific focus or intention of meditation may shift with each stage, but its value remains constant throughout the journey.

Journaling: Listed on page 200, it's a core practice that's supportive across all phases and wounds.

Phase: All Phases

Wound: All Wounds

Journaling is a core spiritual practice that can provide clarity, emotional release, and insights throughout every stage of your journey. Its role can evolve from processing thoughts, to asking questions, to supporting deep transformation, to recording spiritual growth and intuitive insights, to anchoring new ways of being. It is a core practice across each of the wounds to gain clarity and insights into root causes as well as processing the healing of those wounds.

Supporting New Neural Pathways: Listed on page 177, these are great practices throughout your journey, but they're especially supportive in:

Phase: Goo, Expansion, Integration

Wound: All Wounds

The practices of mindfulness, gratitude, and movement can be especially supportive in the later stages, as this is where we are more ready and open to create those new ways of thinking. These practices are also supportive for each of the wounds.

Chanting: Listed on page 225, chanting is a practice you can't go wrong with, but it is extra beneficial for:

Phase: Expansion, Integration

Wound: Body, Connection, Witch

Chanting, or singing, to find your voice is especially powerful during the expansion phase for deepening connection and self-expression, and in the integration phase for sustaining our authentic voice and power. This practice supports both healing and the emergence of our true voice as we move through and beyond the most intense phases of the journey. It is beneficial for all the wounds, but especially Body and Connection, as it creates a vibration within the body to help with connection, as well as the Witch Wound for strengthening the use of our voice.

The Intuitive Strengthening Practices: Listed on page 199, these practices will be supportive throughout your journey.

Phase: All Phases

Wound: All Wounds

You can introduce these practices earlier to begin exploring how your inner wisdom is speaking with you, or for gentle exploration and clarity, but they become especially powerful and transformative as intuition naturally heightens in the later stages and you build trust in your own abilities. These practices will be supportive of each of the four wounds as well.

Boundaries: Listed on page 226, healthy boundaries are always supportive, but they will be very important as you heal and honor yourself, especially in:

Phase: Expansion, Integration

Wound: Body, Connection, Sensitivity

Boundaries are an act of self-love and an important part of healing. In the later phases of your journey, when you've gotten in touch with your own wants and needs again, healthy boundaries will allow you to honor yourself and your relationships. They will be important in healing each of the wounds, but especially the Body and Connection Wounds as you learn to find safety again and honor your sensitive nature.

The Power of Visualization: Listed on pages 91 and 237, visualization can be supportive across all phases and wounds, but especially:

Phase: Expansion, Integration

Wound: All Wounds

Visualization is a powerful tool for releasing blocks, grounding, and charting your path forward. It can be used at any point in time and for healing each of the wounds. It will be especially powerful when you have done the deep inner work and are clear on who you are and what you want.

Now, let's put together your own ritual!

Create Your Ritual

List here the practices that speak to you most and you have determined will support where you are on your own journey.

Decide on what time of day you will commit to putting these into practice, and design your cozy space that you can return to each day.

____

____

____

____

____

Set Your Intention

Your intention is a gentle invitation for yourself. Using the core values, vision, and guiding statement you have outlined for yourself, state your intention for yourself before each practice.

Be Consistent

To truly reap the benefits of your ritual, commit to showing up for yourself. Perhaps start by committing to a short amount of time each day for the next 21 days. However, remember to allow for flexibility; you don't want this to be an added pressure or stress on you. Life can be unpredictable, and it's okay to adapt your practice to fit your schedule. Building in days off or adjusting your ritual when necessary is part of the process.

Navigating Hectic Times

There will be seasons when your attention is needed elsewhere, and that's perfectly normal. When my children were born and I was sleep deprived, you better believe I wasn't waking up to meditate. I found ways to adapt the time I prioritized myself. During very stressful times or in times of transition, we often need our rituals more than ever, but finding the time or energy can be challenging. This is when simplifying your practice can be beneficial. Even the smallest moments of connection or journaling can have a profound impact on our energy and our health.

I am so proud of you for showing up for yourself and recognizing that you deserve to live a life that feels good, one that anchors and supports you. If you implement these practices, I know you will begin to see major shifts in your own life, in the best possible way.

Final Thoughts for the Reader

Suppressing, silencing, pressuring, and criticizing myself was making me sick. But just when I thought I was out of options, spirit appeared at my bedside and reminded me of this:

"You already know."

And they were right.

It was time to stop outsourcing and turn inward. I had access to the answers, the choices, and the healing I was looking for within. Choosing myself, getting uncomfortable, questioning everything I thought I understood, and reclaiming the parts of me I had buried was not an easy process, but it has allowed me to create a life that feels like magic.

This is what I want for you too.

As you awaken to your soul's call and heal your wounds, it can be both a destabilizing and empowering experience. It might feel like your world is crumbling and the foundation is cracking beneath you. But perhaps that foundation wasn't stable enough to hold you and the life that is possible for you in the first place. Recognize the courage and strength it requires to believe in yourself and to rebuild.

If I could impart any wisdom from my own journey, it would be this: You already have all the answers, tools, and wisdom within you. Even if you feel lost, or like you are just missing the key, you're not. Each area of growth, each next step, will be revealed exactly as it should and in divine timing. Expect miracles for yourself; believe that they are possible for you, because they are. Remember your own worth and keep giving yourself permission to grow, heal, and live the life that was always meant for you; one that feels supportive, anchored, and gentle, rather than like a sinking ship.

Remember, the work you do with yourself, when opening up deeper to your own divine connection and inner wisdom, requires you to not simply expand outward into universal consciousness, but to root down into your body, your senses, and yourself. Your experiences have helped shape but not define you, and now you get to decide what is yours to keep and what your story will be for this lifetime.

Some of the practices in this book may seem simple, but don't dismiss their power. Commit to yourself every day, use the framework to create micro habits that support your own journey, and give yourself permission to choose yourself, knowing that you have always had the power.

If you need extra support on your path, visit me at www.danicabanes.com. I'd love to connect!

Until then, I am cheering you on.

So much love to you,
Danica

Bibliography

Chapter 2

Eyal, Maytal. "Self-Silencing Is Making Women Sick." Time.com. October 3, 2023. https://time.com/6319549/silencing-women-sick-essay.

Jack, Dana Crowley. *Silencing the Self: Women and Depression*. Cambridge, MA: Harvard University Press, 1991.

Kannel, W. B. "The Framingham Study: Its 50-Year Legacy and Future Promise." *Journal of Atherosclerosis and Thrombosis* 6, no. 2 (2000): 60–6. https://pubmed.ncbi.nlm.nih.gov/10872616/#:~:text=The%20paper%20also%20found%20that:%20*%20Average,factors%20*%20Genetic%20determinants%20of%20cardiovascular%20disease.

Newport Institute. "Why Young Women Self-Silence and How It Impacts Mental Health." October 26, 2023. https://www.newportinstitute.com/resources/empowering-young-adults/self-silencing.

Chapter 3

Welwood, John. *Toward a Psychology of Awakening: Buddhism, Psychotherapy, and the Path of Personal and Spiritual Transformation*. Boston, MA: Shambhala Publications, 2002.

Chapter 5

Alotiby, Amna. "Immunology of Stress: A Review Article." *Journal of Clinical Medicine* 13, no. 21 (October 25, 2024): 6394. https://doi.org/10.3390/jcm13216394.

Beatie, Melody. *Codependent No More: How to Stop Controlling Others and Start Caring for Yourself.* New York: Spiegel & Grau, 2022.

CoDA.org. "Patterns and Characteristics 2011." Accessed March 24, 2026. https://coda.org/meeting-materials/patterns-and-characteristics-2011.

Sutton, Jeremy. "Mirror Neurons and the Neuroscience of Empathy." PositivePsychology.com. September 7, 2023. https://positivepsychology.com/mirror-neurons.

Johnson, Karan. "The Surprising Power of Daily Rituals." BBC News. September 14, 2021. https://www.bbc.com/future/article/20210914-how-rituals-help-us-to-deal-with-uncertainty-and-stress.

Orloff, Judith. "7 Strategies for Empaths to Heal Trauma & PTSD." Accessed March 24, 2026. https://drjudithorloff.com/7-strategies-for-empaths-to-heal-trauma-ptsd/?srsltid=AfmBOoq3VBYEX6wVfdbBCqQTQX6gygsSwlLPnNDpSRs7cvT_8lnqxN89.

Orloff, Judith. "Empaths, Compassion & Mirror Neurons." Accessed March 24, 2026. https://drjudithorloff.com/empaths-compassion-mirror-neurons.

Orloff, Judith. "The New Science of Empathy and Empaths." Accessed March 24, 2026. https://drjudithorloff.com/the-new-science-of-empathy-and-empaths.

Psychology Today. "Highly Sensitive Person." Accessed March 24, 2026. https://www.psychologytoday.com/us/basics/highly-sensitive-person.

Psychology Today. Psychology Today. "The Secret Lives of Introverts." Accessed March 24, 2026. https://www.psychologytoday.com/us/blog/the-secret-lives-introverts.

Chapter 6

"Water, the Power of Positivity, and Education." *The Fountain Magazine,* no. 132 (November-December 2019). https://fountainmagazine.com/all-issues/2019/issue-132-nov-dec-2019/water-the-power-of-positivity-and-education.

Doyle, Glennon. *Untamed.* New York: The Dial Press, 2020.

Experience Health & Wellness Center. “Sympathetic vs. Parasympathetic and Why They Matter.” April 23, 2021. https://www.efchealth.com/sympathetic-vs-parasympathetic-matter.

Masaru Emoto’s Hado World. “Water Crystals.” February 28, 2014. https://hado.com/ihm/water-crystals.

Matoba, Bob. “Understanding the Sympathetic and Parasympathetic Nervous Systems.” EMS1. July 10, 2020. https://www.ems1.com/ems-products/training-tools/articles/understanding-the-sympathetic-and-parasympathetic-nervous-systems-qOLHBDeIfMiauKoO.

Singh, Manhardeep. *12 Laws of the Universe*. Manhardeep Singh, 2021.

Chapter 7

Balch, Bridget. “Why We Know So Little about Women’s Health.” AAMC. March 26, 2024. https://www.aamc.org/news/why-we-know-so-little-about-women-s-health.

Jainish Patel, Prittesh Patel, Heer Vaghela. “Psychosomatics: Exploring the Role of the Mind-Body Connection in Causing Physical Illnesses.” *Journal of Psychophysiology Practice and Research* 1, no. 1:1–6 (2022).

Lipton, Bruce. *The Biology of Belief 10th Anniversary Edition: Unleashing the Power of Consciousness, Matter & Miracles*. Hay House (2016).

Walker, Pete. “Codependency, Trauma, and the Fawn Response.” Pete Walker.com. January-February 2023. https://pete-walker.com/codependencyFawnResponse.htm.

Zhen-Duah, Jenny, Colombo, Daniella, and Alvarez, Kiara. “Inclusion of Expanded Adverse Childhood Experiences in Research About Racial/Ethnic Substance Use Disparities.” *American Journal of Public Health* (June 20, 2023). https://ajph.aphapublications.org/doi/10.2105/AJPH.2023.307220#:~:text=To%20elucidate%20pathways%20affecting%20the,and%20neglect%2C%20household%20dysfunction).

Pinetree Institute. “The Ace Study.” Accessed March 24, 2026. https://pinetreeinstitute.org/aces.

World Health Organization. "Endometriosis." October 15, 2025. https://www.who.int/news-room/fact-sheets/detail/endometriosis.

Mayo Clinic. "Chronic Stress Puts Your Health at Risk." August 1, 2023. https://www.mayoclinic.org/healthy-lifestyle/stress-management/in-depth/stress/art-20046037.

Chapter 8

Blumberg, Jess. "A Brief History of the Salem Witch Trials." *Smithsonian Magazine*, October 24, 2022. https://www.smithsonianmag.com/history/a-brief-history-of-the-salem-witch-trials-175162489.

Federici, Silvia. *Caliban and the Witch: Women, the Body and Primitive Accumulation*. New York: Autonomedia, 2004. https://med.virginia.edu/perceptual-studies/wp-content/uploads/sites/360/2017/04/REI42-Tucker-James-LeiningerPIIS1550830716000331.pdf.

Larson, Celeste. *Heal the Witch Wound: Reclaim Your Magic and Step into Your Power*. Newburyport, MA: Weiser Books, 2023.

Leininger, B., Leininger, A., and Gross, K. *Soul Survivor: The Reincarnation of a World War II Fighter Pilot*. New York: Grand Central, 2009.

Oren, Guy, Anat Shoshani, Nadra Nasser Samra, et al. "From Trauma to Resilience: Psychological and Epigenetic Adaptations in the Third Generation of Holocaust Survivors." *Nature News*, July 18, 2025. https://www.nature.com/articles/s41598-025-12085–5.

Sociology.Institute. "Analyzing Gender Hierarchies and Social Stratification." August 13, 2025. https://sociology.institute/sociology-of-gender/analyzing-gender-hierarchies-social-stratification.

Sociology.Institute. Tucker, Jim B. "The Case of James Leninger: An American Case of the Reincarnation Type." *EXPLORE* 12, no. 3 (May/June 2016).

Chapter 9

Abhaya Wellness. "The Neuroscience of Mindfulness-Based Stress Reduction." January 16, 2025. https://www.abhayawellness.com/the-neuroscience-of-mindfulness-based-stress-reduction-mbsr/#:~:text=MBSR%20promotes%20neuroplasticity%2C%20the%20brain's%20ability%20to,our%20memory%20and%20emotional%20resilience%20improve%201.

Baldwin, Sarah C. "It Really Is in Your Head, But How Does It Work?" School of Public Health, Brown University, April 24, 2020. https://sph.brown.edu/news/2020-04-24/how-does-mindfulness-work#:~:text=A%20modern%20practice%20based%20on,University%20of%20Massachusetts%20Medical%20School.

Dana, Deb. "What Is a Glimmer?" Rhythm of Regulation. Accessed March 25, 2026. https://www.rhythmofregulation.com/glimmers.

Epstein, Sarah. "What Is a Cycle-Breaker?" Psychology Today. December 1, 2025. https://www.psychologytoday.com/us/blog/between-the-generations/202207/what-is-a-cycle-breaker.

O'Bryan, Amanda. "How to Perform Body Scan Meditation: 3 Best Scripts." PositivePsychology.com. December 4, 2021. https://positivepsychology.com/body-scan-meditation.

Serenity Mental Health Centers. "How Gratitude Rewires the Brain for Wellness." July 6, 2025. https://serenitymentalhealthcenters.com/adhd-blogs/how-gratitude-rewires-the-brain-for-wellness/#:~:text=Recent%20studies%20have%20shown%20that,can%20last%20for%20months%20afterward.

Suzuki, Wendy Suzuki. *Healthy Brain, Happy Life: A Personal Program to Activate Your Brain and Do Everything Better.* New York: Dey Street Books, 2016.

The Society of Analytical Psychology. "The Jungian Shadow." August 12, 2015. https://www.thesap.org.uk/articles-on-jungian-psychology-2/about-analysis-and-therapy/the-shadow/#:~:text=Complementary%20to%20Jung's%20idea%20of,CW9%20paras%20422%20&%20423%5D.

Chapter 10

Gupta, Akhil. "Spiritual Dream Symbols & Meanings: Dream Interpretation Guide." UEF Foundation. May 28, 2025. https://uef.org/dream-interpretation-the-spiritual-dream-symbols-you-should-know-about.

Chapter 11

Perry, G., Polito, V., Sankaran, N., Thompson, W. F. "How Chanting Relates to Cognitive Function, Altered States and Quality of Life." *Brain Sci.* 12, vol 11 (2022 Oct 27):1456. doi: 10.3390/brainsci12111456. PMID: 36358382; PMCID: PMC9688188.

Acknowledgments

When I set out to write this book, I was answering a call from spirit and a gnawing deep in my heart. I didn't know how to write a book, but I was determined to figure it out. From 5 A.M. writing sessions, to joining writing groups, to reading books about writing books, I pieced it together. I wrote *You Already Know* about my own journey of healing self-silencing, but it was actually the process of writing and publishing the book that would stretch me in ways I could not have predicted, asking me to heal on an even deeper level. Something about putting 250 pages of your words and ideas out into the world is like the ultimate *I will not silence myself or shrink in the face of fear.* There were many ups and downs and starts and stops to this journey, but this book would not be possible without the support of a few key people.

First, to my mentor, Pat Longo, who left this world while the book was in progress. You gave me the tools I needed to embrace my mediumship, which in turn taught me to embrace myself. Thank you for believing me. For always meeting me without judgment. For showing me what fearless looks like and what it looks like to come into a lifetime with a soul purpose. Even though you aren't here for the finished product, you continued to guide me from the other side, and I will cherish your support always.

To C.J. Redwine, my dedicated book coach. I believe life has a way of connecting us with the right people, and you were definitely one of those connections. Thank you for seeing this book through from the roughest of outlines to the final period. When I read through the book, I can still hear your voice in my head. The gentle guidance you offered, the different perspectives, the "What if you tried it this way?" Thank you for believing in me and this book from the very beginning.

To Kelly Notaras, thank you for what you bring to the world. Your words helped me believe I actually could write a book. I sat quietly in many of your webinars and writing rooms, scribbling in my journal. To Reid Tracy and the Hay House team for welcoming me with open arms. And to my Hay House editor, Sally Mason-Swaab, for your steady and grounding presence and guidance getting this book out into the world.

And most of all, to my husband, Daniel. Even with all the words I know and how to express them *mostly* eloquently, they could never capture what your love and dedication means to me. Thank you for being the safest space I've ever known and for giving me the opportunity to fall apart so that I could truly find myself. For listening, patiently, every time I doubted my own strength and for always believing in me first so that I could learn how to believe in myself. You are my rock. Forever.

About the Author

Danica Banes is an intuitive guide, psychic medium, writer, and deeply sensitive mom to three humans. It took a decade-long struggle with health issues and relentless messages from spirit for her to realize how she had been abandoning herself, shrinking to fit in, and swallowing her words. In listening to her body and intuitive wisdom, she began walking the path home to herself, finding healing and strength she didn't know was possible. She is still walking that path, step by step. Danica now focuses on guiding and inspiring other sensitive souls to find their own power by building connection to their intuition, their bodies, and their spirit team. She holds workshops, writes a twice-monthly newsletter, and hosts *The Soul's Call* podcast.

Danica lives in New York with her husband, three daughters, and their dog. When she is not writing or wrangling snacks for her kids, she can be found wishing her houseplants alive or sitting very, very still.

danicabanes.com

We hope you enjoyed this Hay House book. If you'd like to receive our online catalog featuring additional information on Hay House books and products, or if you'd like to find out more about the Hay Foundation, please contact:

Hay House LLC, P.O. Box 5100, Carlsbad, CA 92018-5100
(760) 431-7695 or (800) 654-5126
www.hayhouse.com® • www.hayfoundation.org

Published in Australia by:
Hay House Australia Publishing Pty Ltd
18/36 Ralph St., Alexandria NSW 2015
Phone: +61 (02) 9669 4299
www.hayhouse.com.au

Published in the United Kingdom by:
Hay House UK Ltd
1st Floor, Crawford Corner,
91–93 Baker Street, London W1U 6QQ
Phone: +44 (0)20 3927 7290
www.hayhouse.co.uk

Published in India by:
Hay House Publishers (India) Pvt Ltd
Muskaan Complex, Plot No. 3,
B-2, Vasant Kunj, New Delhi 110 070
Phone: +91 11 41761620
www.hayhouse.co.in

HAY
HOUSE